A HISTORY OF LYING

A HISTORY OF LYING

JUAN JACINTO MUÑOZ-RENGEL

Translated from Spanish by Thomas Bunstead

polity

Support for the translation of this book was provided by Acción Cultural Española, AC/E.

AC/E
ACCIÓN CULTURAL
ESPAÑOLA

Polity Press
65 Bridge Street
Cambridge CB2 1UR, UK

Polity Press
111 River Street
Hoboken, NJ 07030, USA

ISBN-13: 978-1-5095-5141-5

A catalogue record for this book is available from the British Library.
Library of Congress Control Number: 2022935230

Typeset in 12.5 on 15pt Dante
by Cheshire Typesetting Ltd, Cuddington, Cheshire
Printed and bound in Great Britain by CPI Group (UK) Ltd, Croydon

For further information on Polity, visit our website:
politybooks.com

Simulation is the essence of the current time. Our politics is simulation, our morality is simulation, simulation is our religion and our science.

Ludwig Feuerbach

That man has always lied, to himself and to others, is indisputable.

Alexandre Koyré

It is only a man's own fundamental thoughts that have truth and life in them.

Arthur Schopenhauer

The poet is a feigner
who is so good at his act
he even feigns the pain
of pain he feels in fact.

Fernando Pessoa

CONTENTS

ACKNOWLEDGEMENTS

My work would not be complete without recording my gratitude to José C. Vales, Jorge Manzanilla and Jaime Rodríguez Uriarte for their brilliant readings.

And, once again, to Ada, also a *conditio sine qua non* of this book.

ONE

Suppose for a moment that the narrator speaking to you now is a fictional construct. Suppose that, to make communication between us possible, I have been obliged to create the illusion of a tone, a voice, a point of view – of a projected identity.

Now suppose that, by extension, everything this narrator says, including these very words, is a lie.

But say we go further still. Suppose – and the verb 'suppose', which comes from the Latin *suppositio*, is not chosen arbitrarily – that everything you have been told over the course of your life is a lie. The history of humankind. The sum of human understanding. The way humans are and how they relate to the world.

Suppose that your memories have been warped by your own mind. Suppose that the story of your life – all that you choose to tell yourself – has also been manipulated by the limitations of memory, by the psychological necessity of self-deceit and by the defence mechanisms of your ego. And therefore, kind reader, that your identity is also a projection.

You, my voice and everything intermediate between us are all lies. Only once this has been accepted will we be in a suitable position to begin communicating. With these premises established, our dialogue can begin.

Because the history of humankind is nothing other than the history of making it up.

MINUS SIX

In the sixth century BC, there lived a Greek philosopher, poet and prophet named Epimenides, who was the first to point out the problem inherent in every narrator, which was the possibility of the unreliable narrator.

Legend has it that Epimenides, retreating once from the midday heat of the Aegean, took refuge in the cool of a cave. Where, if we go along with Diogenes Laertius' account, he slept for fifty-seven years straight. Plutarch, in an attempt to make the story more credible, amends the number, declaring that his nap lasted only fifty years. When he finally awoke, Epimenides found that he had been touched by the gods and that a constant bombardment of divine revelations was raining down on him.

He ran to the city and began throwing truths – like punches – in people's faces. Among many other things, he said:

'All Cretans are liars!'

Bearing in mind that Epimenides was a Cretan, his statement contained quite the dilemma. Because, if Epimenides is a Cretan and all Cretans lie, then, when Epimenides says 'All Cretans are liars', either he himself is lying – which would cast doubt on the truth of the statement – or he is telling the truth, which would automatically mean there is at least one Cretan who is not a liar.

Later philosophers were quick to see the true magnitude of the problem, and even went to some lengths to refine it, in order to highlight further its paradoxical character. Thus, they altered the original premise to 'All claims made by Cretans are always false.' Or to other equivalents such as 'No Cretan ever tells the truth', or simpler ones such as 'This sentence is false', or simply 'I lie.' And so the paradox remained, insoluble, throughout history, leading to dozens of new works and theories in the fields of semantics, logic, mathematics and the philosophy of language.

The problem was finally solved in the twentieth century. Kurt Gödel was among those responsible when he managed to formulate his first incompleteness theorem, which came to show that any recursive axiomatic system that is consistent enough to define natural numbers contains statements that may not be proved or disproved *within* that same system. Bertrand Russell was, too, with his theory of types, which discarded such paradoxical sentences as Epimenides' as being badly formed, that is, as not conforming to the rules of the system of which they themselves are part.

In other words, to understand what happens when I say that 'I lie', we should distinguish between a language and the metalanguage that refers to that language. And in the event that we move up to a higher level or set – as in this moment, as I embark on this loop – between the metalanguage and the meta-metalanguage of that metalanguage, then we will in fact be talking about the meta-meta-metalanguage of the meta-metalanguage of that metalanguage. And so on successively. The semantic paradoxes about the truth in question would then be suppressed for we would be able to see that 'it is true' or 'it is false' do not belong to the same level of metalanguage as 'I lie.'

And, as will be seen, it is in this gift for self-referentiality, in this loop, leap or tail-chasing circle – a quintessentially human gift – that some of the most interesting aspects of our condition are hidden. Some of them will not be so decisive when it comes to humanity's fate – for example, those that relate to the qualities of fashionable literary genres like metafiction and autofiction – but the root of all the great epistemological problems undoubtedly lies in certain other aspects. And among these is the one that concerns us now. Inside this loop, leap or circle, then, there hides the centre of everything: ourselves, and the possibility of fiction and of consciousness.

There will be time to address all these essential questions. I promise we will return to and give a full account of them. With the formal problem of lying – this supposed first obstacle – resolved, however, I think it would be a good idea for you to come with me now. For you to come with me and for us to go back to an even earlier time.

AN EVEN EARLIER TIME: NATURE

Come with me, trust me. I won't deceive you. Most likely, until now, you've been led to believe that lying is something that happens only among our kind, among man- and woman-kind. Perhaps your definition of truth has, roughly, been to do with adapting between what is and what is claimed to be – that is, with an adaptation between reality and thought. And, therefore, it might seem that the truth depends solely on the intervention of the human intellect, which comes into play only with us. At this point, however, we might ask ourselves: so does nature not lie?

Let's go back to the beginning of the world. We don't need to go as far back as the beginning of time, nor even to the period when the planet was forming. It's enough for us to pause in that moment when things began to take the shape we now know, just before the arrival of human beings. Already around us are the forests, rivers, the high mountains and, in the background, the sea, and in them practically all the known animals. Except for us. But let's look a little more closely. Isn't that thing hiding among the branches above a bird that's the exact same colour as the leaves? Don't the feathers of that owl also have the same shape and texture as the rough bark of that tree trunk? Who are they trying to deceive? Their predators, no doubt. And yet, what about that cheetah crouching in the dry grass, with its spots and its straw-coloured fur? Isn't it also using camouflage to fool its prey? Now, let's move away – slowly – mustn't draw attention. Let's go and hunker down on the riverbank, amidst the silence of the world's faint far-off beginnings. Wait. Even here, even in the water, you and I alike have real difficulty picking out those fish on the rocky riverbed, given how faithfully the scales on their backs mimic the shapes of the stones in the water below. And, if we could dive down and somehow get ourselves underneath the fish, we still wouldn't be able to see them, because, as would then become clear, their bellies are just the right colours to blend in with the bright sky above.

The most famous case of crypsis (from *kryptos*, 'cryptic', 'hidden') is perhaps that of the chameleon, which as everyone must know can change skin colour according to circumstance. Despite this, its fame is somewhat undeserved, its transformation not being so complete, nor its control over it so absolute. We would only need to walk around the place where we currently are to discover far more sophisticated specimens: we need look no further than the cuttlefish, which not only changes colour in a matter of seconds, but is at the same time capable of modifying its texture, the entirety of its external structure, and even of generating patterns similar to the shifting seabed which it can then set in motion along its body in the opposite direction to that in which it is actually moving. And not all such strategies are visual. Further on, in that reef over there, its cousins the squids indeed shoot out ink jets to hide themselves, but first and foremost they deceive their natural enemies with the chemistry of their smells.

On the other hand, in addition to all these animals that seek to resemble their environment, everywhere around us we can find abundant examples of mimesis (from *mimos*, 'imitation') in animals trying to look like others, whether those others be dangerous, harmless or repugnant. Like the flies that pretend to be bees, or the snakes that take on the gentle shapes of the coral, or those owls that nest among the rocks and, to protect their eggs, make a sound identical to that of a rattlesnake. And, now that we look closely, the owl that we thought we saw pretending to be part of a tree trunk wasn't in fact even a bird, but rather an owl butterfly with wings outspread, mimicking with astonishing precision the face of an owl. Each of this butterfly's wings shows a marvellous ocellus, or eye-like marking, large and round, of a vivid yellow with black dilated pupils inside. To the point that, in this moment, even though she has concerns entirely her own, we could swear that the non-existent owl is holding our gaze. Such ocelli are not, of course, only found among prey animals like butterflies and fish. Even tigers have the *trompe l'oeil* of an eye outlined on the backs of their ears, in the form of white spots that ward off any attacks from behind.

So, the primeval forest is full of deception.

And, although I've brought you here, at such an untimely hour, maybe you didn't even need to leave your house. Perhaps you could have just observed your pet cat for a few minutes – which is currently motionless, crouched, ready to pounce, and thinks it's in with a chance of catching the sparrow pecking about on the other side of the glass. Doesn't any animal dissemble just by crouching down in this way? Doesn't it try to make others believe that it isn't in the place where it in fact is? Crouching down is always a kind of dissembling; that goes for the victim paralysed by fear, too. But what if you tried to surprise the little hunter by suddenly leaping over to it like a mad person, waving your arms in the air, and getting it to bare its teeth, to hiss at you, fur bristling – wouldn't you say your cat is then pretending to be bigger than it really is? Its arched spine and upstanding fur, would they not again be a form of deception?

All of which means that lying was already there in nature, long before language arose, long before we showed up. You, me or any of our kind.

Imagine the uncertainty of the first primate that found itself plunged into a dream. How perplexed they would have been upon waking. What bewilderment to be suddenly pulled out of that other story, out of that other apparently meaningful reality with all its many images, and to discover oneself back in the cave again, alone, frozen stiff, and the white rabbit they had just caught gone, and their parents, long dead, also now gone. What are dreams but one more huge lie?

What about sex? One of the greatest natural deceptions in the world, and one that cuts from the jungle to the fundamental centre of human society, and still governs our lives today, no matter how aware we may become of our instincts and biological patterns. And it is even greater because it is a double lie. On the one hand, sex deceives us through attraction, making us believe that those legs, that back or that neck are more appealing than the hairy hindquarters of a deer and the sweet musky smell secreted by its glands. Making us think that we are the ones who freely choose one person over another – that tummy, that chest or those ankles, over the swollen, almost exploding belly of the frigate bird, whose intense red colour is irresistible to the females of its species. And then there is the fact that sex deceives us through the illusion of descent. Parents are prey to the illusion that they will be reproduced in their children, who will supposedly be a copy of them, a continuity of their own being, a step towards immortality. But this false promise is a yet another of nature's ruses. Subjects do not reproduce, only species do. Individuals are nothing more than vehicles for genetic code.

Sexual attraction and the need to reproduce, therefore, are deceptions long before the formation of societies. Long before the appearance of the sophisticated idea of love, too, to which I'll have to dedicate a special section later. In the same way that the first lies pre-date language. Even the first conscious lies, those born of shrewd intention – those that have their origin in an intelligent mind, in the capacity to project the future and anticipate what is going to happen – are anterior to language. At some moment in the remote past, for the first time a primate had to emit a cry of alarm that was not genuine. Although it had never happened before, there must have been a specific morning, or perhaps a noontime, when it first occurred to a capuchin monkey to warn of the arrival of a predator with high-pitched screeches and hopping around – but this time not in order to save its companions, but rather to make them all run off, so that it could have the crab it had seen approaching in the grass all to itself. The first semantic lie.

Millions of years later, of course, language as we know it would emerge and lies could then become far more complex and refined, giving rise to art, religions, science and the whole of contemporary culture.

However, attentive reader, I would like you to have noticed not only that there are lies that pre-date human beings, but also that they are above the level of the individual. It is not one owl in particular that chooses to adopt a plumage similar to the tree trunks, nor a single cheetah that decides to turn yellow in the savannah. Even a certain chameleon or a certain cuttlefish does not get to choose. It is in the *species* and not in individuals that the lie resides. It is in nature, in its higher plan, in its inextricable desire for permanence and evolution in some direction, that the will to mislead is embedded. Counterfeiting, manipulation and deception do not require the trifling will of beings endowed with intelligence. The orchid mimics female bees with its labellum, not only imitating their shape, but also replicating their pheromone production, in order that the drones will pollinate it. And it doesn't even have a nervous system.

I assured you that I was not going to deceive you, that you could accompany me risk-free. I lied.

Perhaps you know the anecdote about the writer J. D. Salinger told by his daughter in her memoirs. In a passage from *The Guardian of Dreams*, Margaret Salinger recalls a childhood experience that, because of her tender age, may have been traumatic for her. Father and daughter were sitting in front of their living room window in their home in Cornish, New Hampshire, looking out at the woods and high mountains, the crops, the animals and the farms. Then the writer got up, waved his hand over the window in a gesture meant to indicate erasing each of the shapes beyond it, and said:

'All this is maya, an illusion. Isn't it wonderful?'

Well, this is what's just happened to us. Nothing that you and I have seen is real: not the forests, not the mountains, not the sea, the owl, the cheetah, the fish, the colours or smells. They were necessary just so that we could understand each other. Do you see? They aren't here now.

Nothing that is beyond us, nothing that comes to us through the senses is true. Or, at least, that momentous leap is one we haven't yet been able to make. For the moment, we are still locked in here, inside ourselves. And everything else is illusion.

TWO

In a way, the lie is a question of two.

At least two opposed entities are needed for one to make the other believe that what is is not. Or two subjects; or, on one side, reality and, on the other, a subject with a minimal capacity for perception. Strictly speaking, however, I am afraid (very afraid) that these two sides of the coin come down to only oneself and the world. Perhaps, reader of these lines, in this search for the truth there is only space for two extremes: you and everything else.

Even in the very way the problem has been articulated, duality has been present from the beginning. We need look no further than the two principal traditions in the history of philosophy, initiated by Plato and Aristotle. In Plato's case, he brought truth itself into existence: Truth is unique, perfect, eternal and immutable, and exists independently of the mind in the World of Ideas. Whereas Aristotle, moving away from identifying truth and reality, grounded it more in earthly things and limited it to a mere property of certain statements: 'To say of what is that it is not, or of what is not that it is, is false, while to say of what is that it is, and of what is not that it is not, is true.' Aristotle was ahead of his time here, inaugurating, in the fourth book of his *Metaphysics*, the semantic conception of truth, and bringing us closer to ideas about adaptation or correspondence. And yet, both traditions have turned out to be dead ends, ultimately leading us back to the point where we started. Ourselves. The Aristotelian meaning withstood the passing of the centuries, being assimilated over time into nominalism, empiricism, materialism, structuralism and deconstructionism, before throwing us into this relentlessly sceptical world in which we now exist. Platonism, on the other hand, was fervently embraced, for its own ends, by Christianity, thanks to Saint Augustine's maxim establishing God as the only possible source of truth. Centuries later, Nietzsche – one of the three great masters of scepticism – would refer to this concept of truth as the conspiracy engineered by Socrates, Plato and the Judaeo-Christian tradition to chain man in the prison of reason and keep him locked away from his passions. The invention of truth would be, in Nietzschean terms, the greatest lie of the Greco-Latin culture and of the West, a trap concocted by cowards who feared life, with the net result that our vital instincts were left behind. Platonism did try to escape the mire, on many occasions, with various bids to integrate Aristotelian concepts into its theoretical corpus, beginning with the work of Thomas Aquinas within Scholasticism itself, and continuing with the likes of Descartes, Malebranche and Leibniz, and their truths of reason and truths in fact.

Out of these – and, more generally, out of all the minds in history – the French philosopher René Descartes is one who would undoubtedly submit the truth to the most stringent of tests. It's with him that we passed the point of no return.

Descartes himself said that from a very young age, he noticed that he had become used to accepting a certain proportion of false opinions, and that therefore everything he built on them in later years could only be considered doubtful and debatable. So when he judged the moment right, having reached intellectual maturity and in the exile of his long and quiet stay in Holland, always by the heat of his stove, he decided to face the task of his life: to reject systematically each and every one of his beliefs and find at least one unquestionable truth on which to build. To get past this initial phase of scepticism, he first wrote his *Discourse on Method*, in which he established the rules for correct thinking, and those aimed at discovering truths from analysis and synthesis. But, not content with this, and always abiding by his own rules, four years later he published his *Metaphysical Meditations*. And it is in the first of these meditations that, perhaps without actually guessing the consequences of what he was about to do, and with an iron will, he established his form of methodological scepticism, otherwise known as Cartesian doubt.

As a first step, in order to take up a position of possible maximum doubt, and having observed that the senses can at times mislead us but we might not know when, Descartes took the decision to discard everything that comes to us by way of perception. Second, noting that, even after putting aside sense data, it was difficult for him to deny that he was where he was, sitting where he was sitting, in front of the embers with his comfortable, barely creased robe on and papers in his hands, he asked himself: and what if this pleasant warmth on my feet has made me fall asleep and I am dreaming? This second premise was even more radical than the previous one, because the impossibility of confidently distinguishing between wakefulness and sleep threw just about everything into question. Can I be completely sure that I am in this room? Can I not perhaps doubt the existence of my own body, of any pain I feel or any other stimuli, as well as these hands I see balled up into fists at the end of my arms? Only one thing remained that still seemed to resist the dream hypothesis: whether we are asleep or awake, two plus three will always equal five, and a square will always have four sides. Mathematical truths stand above any method of doubt. Any at all? It is then that the rationalist philosopher, in his search for the unquestionable truth, brought all his artillery to bear with his third hypothesis, that of the Evil Genius or the Deceiving God. What if an almighty god had created me with a kind of intelligence that always kept me in error, so that everything true seemed false to me, and everything false seemed true? Viewed through the lens of this assumption, nothing we know would ever be safe again.

Only one thing – though it was barely anything – was left standing after such a cataclysm. After submitting to so many doubts, the castaway Descartes, exhausted and confused in the middle of a devastated universe, finally finds a single certainty to hold on to: in all cases, even in the face of the most drastic suppositions, there must be someone doing the doubting, something capable of being deceived. Someone who thinks and therefore exists – or, in other words, his famous 'cogito ergo sum.' His island.

Starting from this minimal unit of the thinking subject, René Descartes would propose an out-and-out reconstruction of reality. This would mean first affirming the existence of a few ideas innate to that self: the very idea of existence, the idea of thought itself, and the idea of infinity. Next, he would link the most questionable of the three, the idea of infinity, with the idea of God, and attempt to prove its existence. To which end he would argue that an infinite, eternal, independent, omniscient and omnipotent idea could not come from me, seeing as I am finite, but must rather have some external cause. Then, once the existence of God was proven, it would be easy for him to re-establish the existence of the world: an omnipotent God cannot be a deceiver, because deceit depends on an error, a defect, a deficiency of being, and it is therefore impossible that it should be the doing of an all-powerful divine entity whose actions always have a real effect in and of themselves. And if God exists and is infinitely good, He would never allow me to deceive myself into believing that the world exists if it did not. Therefore, the world exists.

Thus, it was via an act of faith that the founder of rationalism demonstrated the existence of the world.

Descartes deployed countless tricks in order to get beyond that first, solipsistic state, to elude the isolation of the 'cogito' and rebuild reality's other parts. We could stop to analyse whether the idea of infinity is truly clear and different, as required by the rules of his method; or if, in order to demonstrate the existence of God, the philosopher did not in fact abuse Saint Anselm's old, failed ontological argument; or if, with his reasoning, he was not in fact placing a limit on the omnipotence of God, claiming that, even if He wanted to, He is incapable of deceiving us. A little historical perspective, however, is all we need to see that Descartes's notions of goodness, and of lies as defects of being, were clearly based on the Platonic–Christian conceptual framework, and because of them he was prompted to rely on the very prejudices he had made such efforts to get away from. We could, in short, continue to question in turn all the logical incongruities provoked by the Cartesian meditations that followed on from his scepticism. But, finally, we cannot simply dismiss the most awful possibility: that there is something out there that deceives us. We have plenty of evidence to believe that reality deceives us and that in nature, which is prior to humanity, lies are actually inherent.

This is why, once we have accepted Descartes's methods as valid, but then see that their outcomes are untrue, we once more find ourselves in this place, trapped.

REALITY AS SIMULACRUM

I will think that the sky, the air, the earth, the colours, all figures and all sounds – and every other exterior thing – are nothing but illusions and deceptions made expressly for the purpose of fooling me. I will consider myself devoid of hands, eyes, flesh, blood. I will attempt to remain unmovable in this conviction and, should I never find my way to any truths by such means, at least I will be in a position to suspend judgement. This is what I shall do. This decision, however, will turn out to be more arduous than expected. It will require perseverance and discipline, such that the indolence of the days will end up dragging me back into the habits of my ordinary life. And, like a slave that dreams of enjoying an imaginary freedom, when I then begin to suspect my freedom a dream, I will fear to wake. And I shall conspire with all the indulgent illusions in order to go on being fooled, to remain in darkness . . .

No, these are not my words. Even though I missed out the quotation marks. And neither do they belong to a big-budget futuristic dystopia that attempts to show us how everything we understand to be reality could have been generated by a technology belonging to another civilization, or some artificial intelligence or invading species. They are a paraphrase of something Descartes wrote in 1641, after putting himself through the hypothesis of a malignant spirit. This was when he still thought himself capable of finding a way out of the place he was assigning to all thinking subjects.

And from then until our present moment, the awareness of the idea that life is an illusion has only intensified. To the point that it now pervades our entire culture.

Admittedly, the notion of reality as simulacrum has been a feature of philosophy since antiquity. It was there in eastern thought via the concept of maya – in the sacred texts of the Upanishads and the school of Vedanta, maya is the illusion, the world as appearance or the self of phenomena, as against the Absolute, the transcendent Being or Brahman; the latter is hidden behind the veil of the former, and this is why empirical phenomena may be entirely unreal. And it was present in Plato, from the moment he separated the world of the senses from that other World of Ideas, giving rise to a vivid and memorable theory of knowledge rendered in the famous allegory of the cave. I will repeat it once more, conscious though I am of its prominence in the history of philosophy and the fact you will likely know of it already. Plato asks us to imagine a group of men inside a cave, held captive there since a young age with their legs and necks in chains, so that they have only ever been able to look straight ahead. Behind them is a wall separating them from the rest of the cave, from another group of men who have all manner of different objects in their hands, from the fire that is the single source of light, and from the light coming from the cave mouth as well. These men in chains have never had any contact with the outside world, their only interaction with reality being the flickering shadows from the fire on the cave wall which, though only the distorted projections of man-made objects, they would think were completely real – they would think the sounds echoing around were coming from them, and would establish entirely fictitious causal relations between them. These prisoners – prevented from walking about and, indeed, from contemplating the outside world by the light of day without being blinded, condemned only ever to put forward weak conjectures about reality and to embrace a set of beliefs utterly removed from the truth of things – are us.

So the suspicion that what we call reality is nothing more than a ruse has been with us since the beginning: the achievement of Cartesian doubt was to catalyse it. Descartes's thought not only gave rise to rationalism: it would very soon fling us into the arms of subjective idealism, no less, which would find an ardent foundational proponent in the Irishman George Berkeley – Bishop Berkeley. He went as far as declaring that matter does not exist outside the mind and that things only are to the extent that there is someone to perceive them. *Esse est percipi.* Further down the line, one of the consequences of this unfolding line of thought would be phenomenology and, finally, postmodernity. All modern and contemporary philosophy is impregnated by this feeling of treading a path between illusions, or by the impression of being unable to avoid multiplying them the further we advance.

Come the twentieth century, Bertrand Russell managed to express the shadow of this scepticism with an equally vivid and evocative image. He did so in the first chapter of his *An Outline of Philosophy* (1927), going back to a supposition he had initially articulated in the ninth lecture of his *The Analysis of Mind* (1921):

> There is no logical impossibility in the hypothesis that the world sprang into being five minutes ago, exactly as it then was, with a population that 'remembered' a wholly unreal

past. There is no logically necessary connection between events at different times; therefore nothing that is happening now or will happen in the future can disprove the hypothesis that the world began five minutes ago.[1]

And, similarly to what happened with philosophy, in the ambit of fiction – which is at least as, if not more, capable of transforming our world – the idea of reality as a simulacrum was conceived thousands of years ago. Its first appearance might also have been in the East, in the form of an anecdote that would go on to become a haiku and, finally, something resembling a very short short story. There is an account from some Taoist scholars in around 4 BC of Zhuang Zi – also sometimes transcribed as Chuang Tse or Chuang Tzu – having a dream of being a butterfly happily flitting from flower to flower. In the morning, however, he awoke in confusion, because the dream had been so intense that, while it lasted, he had completely forgotten who he was. His students asked him:

'Master, we have never seen you sad before. What is the matter today?'

The sage turned to them, a faraway look in his eyes, as though having just come back from another world.

'I have a problem for you all, one that I want you to try to resolve.'

'Okay, what is it?'

'I dreamed in the night that I was a butterfly.'

His students burst out laughing, thinking he was joking.

'But now you are awake. What's the problem?'

'Pay attention. The problem is this: if I am able to sleep and in my dreams turn into a butterfly, what is there to

[1] Bertrand Russell, *An Outline of Philosophy*. London: Routledge, 2009.

stop the exact opposite from happening? A butterfly could in the same way fall asleep and dream that it has turned into Zhuang Zi. So then tell me, have I really dreamed of being a butterfly, or is the butterfly now dreaming of being Zhuang Zi?'

Accounts like this clearly suggest that the sceptical hypothesis of the dream has antecedents far back in every culture. In the Arabic tradition, for instance, this questioning of what is real would have an equivalent in one of the tales from *A Thousand and One Nights* entitled: 'The Ruined Man Who Became Rich Again through a Dream'. While in western literature we could talk about anything from Pindar – 'man is a dream of a shadow' – to Shakespeare – 'we are such stuff as dreams are made on; and our little life is rounded with a sleep'. Or from Sophocles – 'a human being is only breath and shadow' – to Calderón de la Barca, who, in the climax of his play *Life Is a Dream*, draws out the illusory nature of reality in Segismundo's famous lines:

> What is life? An illusion,
> A shadow, a fiction,
> And the greatest good is small;
> For all of life is a dream,
> And dreams, are only dreams.[2]

Curiously enough, Lewis Carroll chooses to conclude *Through the Looking-Glass* with an almost identical line: 'Life, what is it but a dream?' After delving into the world of dream and paradox in *Alice in Wonderland*, with which he made his name, the country parson and brilliant

[2] Pedro Calderón de la Barca, *La Vida Es Sueño / Life Is a Dream: A Dual-Language Book*. New York: Dover Publications Inc., 2003.

mathematician came up with a sequel in which he moved on to the world of speculation, shifting up a level the problems posed while persisting with the idea of dreams within dreams. In chapter 4, Alice encounters Tweedledum and Tweedledee, who proceed to show her that she herself is no more than a trifle in the King's dream:

> 'He's dreaming now,' said Tweedledee: 'and what do you think he's dreaming about?'
>
> Alice said, 'Nobody can guess that.'
>
> 'Why, about you!' Tweedledee exclaimed, clapping his hands triumphantly. 'And if he left off dreaming about you, where do you suppose you'd be?'
>
> 'Where I am now, of course,' said Alice.
>
> 'Not you!' Tweedledee retorted contemptuously. 'You'd be nowhere. Why, you're only a sort of thing in his dream!'
>
> 'If that there King was to wake,' added Tweedledum, 'you'd go out – bang! – just like a candle!'[3]

Jorge Luis Borges, among many other things, became the leading disseminator of the anecdote about Zhuang Zi and the butterfly – ahead of the likes of Octavio Paz and Lezama Lima – when he included it in several of his own writings, as well as in *The Book of Fantasy*, which he co-edited alongside Adolfo Bioy Casares and Silvina Ocampo. His has gone on to become perhaps the most well-known version of all.[4] *The Book of Fantasy* also happened to take

[3] Lewis Carroll, *Through the Looking-Glass*. London: Macmillan, 1871.

[4] 'Chuang Tzu dreamt that he was a butterfly flittering and fluttering around as he pleased. Suddenly he woke up and realized that he was Chuang Tzu. But he did not know whether he was Chuang Tzu dreaming that he was a butterfly or a butterfly dreaming he was Chuang Tzu': 'The Dream of the Butterfly', in

in the above-mentioned Carroll fragment. Compared to the philosophers and writers so far mentioned, Borges felt just as assailed by the idea of life as an illusion – if not more – to the extent that it would be excessive to list each and every one of his poems, stories, articles and essays in which it features. His works even include a *Book of Dreams*, where he once again gathers together these passages, with the intention of compiling all the great dreams of humanity, from the first prophetic dreams of the Far East to the latest fictional games in his current time. Nonetheless, it is perhaps with one of his own short stories, 'The Circular Ruins', that he best achieves this old intention of presenting life as a dream, with a protagonist who sets himself the task of dreaming a man: 'He wanted to dream him with minute integrity and insert him into reality.'[5] And, little by little, through the complex structure of the story, Borges manages to project the architecture of a universe composed of men – or gods – that dream one another into existence.

He also does something similar in the short text 'Everything and Nothing', which is dedicated to the figure of Shakespeare. In its final lines, when the English poet who brought to life so many characters finds himself close to death, knowing that God is near, he dares to ask:

> 'I who have been so many men in vain want to be one man only, myself.'
>
> The voice of God answered him out of a whirlwind:
>
> 'Neither am I what I am. I dreamed the world the way you dreamed your plays, dear Shakespeare. You are one

Jorge Luis Borges, Silvina Ocampo and Adolfo Bioy Casares, eds., *The Book of Fantasy*, tr. Herbert A. Giles [1926]. London: Viking/Penguin, 1988.

[5] Jorge Luis Borges, *Collected Fictions*. New York: Penguin Books, 1999.

> of the shapes of my dreams: like me, you are everything and nothing.'[6]

It is worth clarifying that, though he uses Him as theme and fictional device on innumerable occasions, Borges never goes as far as affirming the existence of God. Really, all of Borgesian thought oscillates within something resembling the following dilemma: is life something that somebody dreams – somebody who could only finally be the entity we vaguely conceive of as God – or is it rather a dream that dreams itself?

This said, there is still another of the Argentinian genius's stories that is of special pertinence here. A text that moves away from the hypothesis of the dream and that, nonetheless, represents far more exactly the state of play throughout the postmodern era: the way in which culture – the hyperreal human construct forever floating about us – has ended up engulfing everything that we intuitively previously understood to be authentic, as well as our fragile contact with the world. In the story 'Tlön, Uqbar, Orbis Tertius', a secret society of scientists and great men has dedicated itself to the making of an encyclopaedia, the first ever about the planet Tlön. That is, its members are entirely consumed in the laborious creation of a history, a metaphysics, a theology, the algebra, geometry, language and geography, of a non-existent planet. And the documentation of this fictitious planet, all that is known about it, just keeps growing and growing, to the point where it begins to affect the real world. And to the point where Tlön, along with its congenitally idealist inhabitants – who, like Berkeley, reject all materialism as mental aberration

[6] Ibid.

– ends up actually taking the place of the known world, superseding it entirely.

In an unsettlingly similar way, as we go through the process of adding new knowledge and new fictions to the sphere of our cultural pool, we also place new layers over the top of our model of reality, so that it comes to resemble less and less closely that which it previously was.

Borges's great friend and long-time collaborator Adolfo Bioy Casares, the other editor – alongside his wife, Silvina Ocampo – of *The Book of Fantasy*, for his part also designed a powerful artefact of simulated reality. In his novel *The Invention of Morel*, a fugitive holed up on a radiation-contaminated desert island suddenly discovers the impossible presence of a group of tourists. Unable to work out what they're up to, and impelled by his curiosity to begin spying, he witnesses them engaging in certain odd activities – like trying to warm themselves up though the weather is suffocatingly hot. There will also be moments when he sees two moons and two suns in the sky. There is only one possible explanation after a long series of strange phenomena: one of the tourists – Morel – has invented a machine capable of reproducing reality.

From our current position, we might think that anyone presented with the results of Morel's machine might not feel so different from the people who attended the Lumière Brothers' first public exhibition one January evening in 1896, when *The Arrival of a Train at La Ciotat* was projected in the Grand Café de Paris. Except that, in the latter case, it was in three all-enveloping dimensions.[7]

[7] If it hadn't been, this famous episode in the history of cinema would seem like yet another of the many lies that go to form our vision of the world. According to Martin Loiperdinger, in spite of countless references in recent decades both in the media and in mainstream manuals of cinema history –

And it would not be possible to conclude this survey of the ways in which our certainties on the nature of reality have progressively sunk beneath our feet without mentioning arguably the most influential sci-fi author in contemporary culture: Philip K. Dick, of whom another master of the genre, Ursula K. Le Guin, said, 'We have our own homegrown Borges.' His influence on our current way of conceiving the world cannot be measured through his written work alone, something that always soaks into the social fabric more slowly; we must instead consider the slew of screen adaptations of his work, which have guaranteed his unique vision a far greater and almost instantaneous impact on society. Dick's work is shot through with sceptical treatments of reality as a knock-off, a simulated version.

For more than two decades – with a sequence that would go from *Eye in The Sky* (1957) to the *Valis* trilogy (1982), by way of innumerable short stories and further novels such as *Time Out of Joint* (1959), *The Penultimate Truth* (1964), *Ubik* (1969) and *Flow My Tears, the Policeman Said* (1974) – his work circled around two enduring concerns: what reality is, and what constitutes an authentic human being. Whether through heavy doses of technology or drugs, these two interrelated themes were a constant in his

which say the spectators felt 'fear, terror, even panic', 'gripped the armrests of their seats', 'went running out of the hall for fear that the train was going to run them over' – no reports exist from the time that suggest any such reaction. Which means that this myth of contemporary society would be better off relegated to the realm of historical fantasy.

On the other hand, nor would *The Arrival of a Train at La Ciotat* be a documentary piece. It would, in reality, be a film orchestrated by Louis Lumière, a proto-filmic scene in which the purported travellers are actually extras – recognizable acquaintances of the Lumières who have been instructed not to look at the camera and to act naturally. A lie on top of another lie.

output, which, as the author himself declared at the end of the 1970s in a lecture entitled 'How to Build a Universe that Doesn't Fall Apart Two Days Later', always turned on questions about what we are and what it is that surrounds us, the latter also being what we call the not-self, or the empirical world of phenomena.

The protagonist in his novel *Time Out of Joint*, one among any number of his characters who could serve as an example, believes himself to be living in 1959 in a quiet residential area in the US. But, because of certain premonitory faculties, and because of the different anomalies that keep on cropping up, he begins to suspect that his world is not real at all. On attempting to flee the city where he lives, and having overcome all manner of absurd obstacles, he discovers that the date is actually 1998 – only for his captors to detain him and erase his memory. During a second escape attempt, this time accompanied by his brother-in-law – who, along with everybody else, is conspiring in the enormous masquerade – he will learn that his idyllic city is entirely constructed on the basis of his childhood memories and his dreams, as a way of protecting him from a future where war breaks out with lunar colonists. In this particular plot, the powers that be are represented by the military high command, who use aspects of the protagonist's personality to predict where the enemy's next nuclear bombs are going to fall.

In all likelihood you will have noticed the many coincidences here with *The Truman Show*, the well-known film directed by Peter Weir – in 1998, no less. Nonetheless, it isn't the only one of Dick's works aimed at lifting the veil on reality's big lie, and that has had a huge impact on the way we perceive the world around us today. The American writer had the ability to wreak genuine havoc in our culture with stories barely twenty pages long. Think, for example, of the plot in the story 'We Can Remember It for You Wholesale' (1966), whose main character is desperate to travel to Mars but doesn't have the necessary funds. So, instead, he pays a trip to a company called Rekal Inc. for memory implants of having been to the red planet as a secret agent. Problems arise when they try to modify his memory, only to discover that he has indeed been working for Earth's government as a secret agent and that they have wiped all confidential information from his memory. At this point, the reader of the story – and doubtless of these lines as well – can already intuit the vertiginous loop that opens up beneath him: from here on, it is going to be difficult to distinguish whether everything that's happening is real or just part of the holiday package bought by the client. The plot of the popular film *Total Recall*, directed by Paul Verhoeven and with Arnold Schwarzenegger in the main role, will also have been easily recognizable, and yet the story's influence is possibly even greater, and it would not be until the latter half of the 1990s that the true effect of this and other short stories of his would be fully felt, in films with a global reach that would include the likes of *Twelve Monkeys* (1995), *Strange Days* (1995), the Japanese *Ghost in the Shell* (1995), *Open Your Eyes* (1997) (though director Alejandro Amenábar has never recognized Dick as a direct influence), *Gattaca* (1998), *Dark City* (1998), *eXistenZ* (1999), *Level 13* (1999), *Being John Malkovich* (1999) and, probably above and beyond all of these, *The Matrix* (1999).

This last example has undoubtedly become the standout reference point for ideas about virtual, computer-generated realities. *The Matrix* – which abounds with references to works such as *Alice in Wonderland* – has become a cult movie, known by many as the Digital Bible, a huge success with legions of followers that has generated its very own strain of popular philosophy centred around the perception of reality as a simulacrum.[8]

It was the culmination of the domino effect prompted by Dick's thinking at the end of the century, the virus introduced by him and by Borges spreading to its full extent into the heart of postmodernity, which was already rife with scepticism and doubt. For all that, its repercussions would continue well into the following decade.[9]

---

[8] The main character in *The Matrix*, Neo, receives a message on his computer that leads him to discover the unreality of the world he is living in: 'Wake up, Neo . . . The Matrix has you . . . Follow the white rabbit . . .' And so begin his attempts to track down a hacker named Morpheus who, like the rabbit of Alice's dream, will serve as his guide, warning him: 'This is your last chance. After this, there is no turning back . . . You take the blue pill, the story ends. You wake up and believe . . . whatever you want to believe. You take the red pill . . . you stay in wonderland . . . and I show you just how deep the rabbit hole goes. Remember . . . all I'm offering you is the truth: nothing more.'

And there is Arnold Schwarzenegger's character in *Total Recall*, who, nine years before, was offered the red pill and told that it was a symbol of his desire to go back to reality.

And then, if we go a long way back in history, the character of the Oracle – who in *The Matrix* will be revealed as an AI program – could represent not only Lewis Carroll's Cheshire Cat or Caterpillar, but also the Oracle of Delphi who, according to Plato's *Apologia*, provided insights for Plato's master Socrates, thereby also irrevocably changing the destiny of the creator of the cave allegory.

[9] In the form of the two sequels, *The Matrix Reloaded* (2003) and *Matrix Revolutions* (2003), and in movies like *Donnie Darko* (2001), *Eternal Sunshine of the Spotless Mind* (2004) and Christopher Nolan's *Inception* (2010), or the entire series of *Westworld*, in which a passage by Dick would not be at all out of place: 'Almost at once, Mr. Garson Poole discovered that his reality consisted of punched tape passing from reel to reel in his chest. Fascinated, he began to fill in some of the punched holes and add new ones. Immediately, his world changed. A flock of ducks flew through the room when he punched one new hole in the tape. Finally he cut the tape entirely, whereupon the world disappeared' (Philip K. Dick, 'How to Build a Universe that Doesn't Fall Apart Two Days Later', 1978).

The era in which we live is flooded by these images, which spread extremely easily. And our perception of what is real depends on our iconic legacy – the way in which we learn to interpret images and how we construct our identity, both individual and collective; the way we write or rewrite our history; and how traditions, legends, the popular imaginary, biases and prejudices take shape. Ideas accumulate, evolve and transform around human beings. Thus has it always been; for all that, we still have not succeeded in stepping beyond our own minds or providing evidence for everything else in the world – nonetheless, none of us ever thinks or creates in isolation. Not even the greatest ahead-of-their-time genius has done so, for every idea always builds on so many previous ideas, giving rise to the complex framework of our accumulated knowledge within our systems of writing and the conglomeration that is everyone else's minds. In spite of which, for the moment, everyone else's minds remain nothing more than conjecture and a continuation of my own subjectivity.

And so we find ourselves always at the border between worlds.

In a constant and fragile equilibrium between the physical and the metaphysical. Between the self and the other. Between perceptions and things in themselves. Between appearances and that which is – or that which supposedly is.

Falling over ourselves to weave our network of fictions, with the abyss of purest nothing there beneath our feet.

THE FIRST BIG LIE

When the naked ape appears in the world, its greatest attribute is its inventiveness, its capacity for fiction. It is fiction alone – not strength, size, toughness or speed – that allows it to raise itself up above other species. Like the tiger's claws and the snake's venom, our capacity for making things up is the evolutionary trait that has enabled our survival, adaptation and, finally, mastery of our environment.

To lie, to deceive, to simulate – these above everything else have enabled us to keep going as a species. To poeticize, to narrate, to tell stories, to conjecture, to falsify; in the knowledge process, these are fundamental. Mistakes, strategy, manipulation, supposition, speculation, metaphor, hypothesis – these are some of the many faces of our way of being in the world. They are how we construct the world. If scientists and philosophers were not in a position to cast the net of their hypotheses – which are one of the shapes that lies can take – they would never catch anything worthwhile. In the same way, we need literature to give an account of ourselves, to relate the events of our lives to ourselves, to explain things that have happened in history, and theories, within the framework of a meaningful narrative. Identity, and life itself, cannot be understood except as a tale.

And yet, at the same time, not even the most sceptical person, as much as she or he is conscious of all this and believes that everything around them is false – for all that they may be aware that their entire stock of knowledge is mere presumption – not even they can just reject out of hand what their senses tell them. Nobody in their right mind finds it possible not to empathize with their fellow humans, or to ignore physical pain.

All of which means: no sooner have we appeared than we are dragged into doing what we know best. The first thing we did was to lie, to speculate, to misdirect, to launch into our first great hypothesis: the existence of the world.

MAGICAL AND MYTHICAL THINKING

Though we are better liars than any other species, our thinking – like so many other evolutionary traits – is not without its defects. A male elk's huge antlers serve as a weapon and a way of demonstrating its virility to the females, but it requires a huge outlay of energy to grow 3 metres and 30 kilos of great branching horn year on year, and having to carry that weight around on your head during the months of courtship is not precisely ideal. The long thin beak of the hummingbird enables it to extract the nectar from flowers, while that of the sword-billed hummingbird – at 12 centimetres long – reaches where none of its competitors' can; and yet the beak's length also means that the bird has to keep its head up all the time, to avoid toppling over, and – because the beak is actually longer than its body – that it can never preen or delouse itself. In the same way, human intelligence is useful in helping us to survive and source enough food to eat, but it has had countless other repercussions. And not all of them are beneficial.

The essence of human thought is the ability to project. And this includes the projection of every kind of illusion, fancy and misapprehension onto reality.

This is why the first thing humankind does when it emerges as a species – with no convincing evidence, and on the basis of nothing but a few intuitions – is to declare its faith in the world's existence. That first supposition was nothing but a hypothesis – a transitory one, as all are. Nonetheless, even though over the centuries we have formulated an incontestable logical refutation, and in spite of the reams of scientific data confirming that the universe is nothing like our perception of it, we still persist with it. We live, yes, in a state of constant scepticism, and, as we have seen, the twenty-first century is trapped in a sphere of images that show reality to be a simulacrum, but neither you nor I is capable of refuting that which comes to us via our senses – our very nature prevents us from doing so. We don't walk naked down the street as though other minds did not exist, we don't get up in the morning thinking that perhaps the laws of physics might have changed and we might now be able to fly, and – though it makes not the slightest difference to our feeling that we are connected to reality by a thread – we don't go and jump out of the window to demonstrate that matter doesn't really exist. On the contrary, we will remain stuck inside our little situations – this problem that is getting in our way, a certain pain, distress or illness that is being visited on us or someone close to us – and we know that when we wake up the next day, it will still be there, waiting for us. And we will clearly distinguish between the various levels of our fictions: the resistant, solid ones, as with physical objects; those that are part of shared culture; and those that are intimate and belong exclusively to our private mental universe.

The next thing in the early days of our era that the babbling human will do – not content with the haste of that first declaration – will be to launch into a second grand hypothesis: the existence of identity.

And, around this thinking self, this dot of lucidity – this minimal awareness that Descartes will later go on to demonstrate irrefutably – all sorts of entelechies will begin to accumulate. And that is all they will be: delusions, fallacies, semblance upon semblance. Because the only thing that makes this indivisible subjectivity seem to possess a complex personal identity is its continuity in time. Nothing more. And in order to construct this psychological continuity, all we have is our memory, which is fallible; which works on the basis of images, imprecise copies, whether they arise out of our imagination or our experience; which imposes a random chronological order and which could ultimately have been implanted in us – as in Russell's supposition or Dick's short story – just a few minutes ago, for all that it seems to contain years of recollections.

And in this way, the human being, with its shiny new individual identity, blessed with supposed continuity, with a past, with a character and its very own autobiographical story, looks around, and smiles. Its work has only just begun. Indeed, like other advanced mammals, it finds itself in a world that existed before it came into being. But, unlike them, humans are not content with this prefabricated world as it is, but are driven by their principal evolutionary trait to go beyond that and build an intermediate world all for themselves.

So begins the third phase of our fictionalizing process, in which we are still immersed to this day: the construction of our pyramid in the air.

What happens is that, in this state – naked as it is, exposed to danger, buffeted by chance events and pressing needs, fearing for its future, having to depend on its cunning intelligence alone – there is no choice but to turn to magical thinking. In its determination to rebuild the world, weakness and fear will therefore lead it to choose the path of least resistance. When the human being is ruled by the need to control chance and nature, in the face of which it feels so powerless and small, it will seek to trick the secret forces it imagines hiding behind them. Following the logic of magical thinking, it will deduce that something which happened once under certain conditions is bound to happen again should those conditions recur. And the deficiencies of our judgement will be fully on show when we decide that these conditions include not only the actual causes of the event, but coincidental factors as well.

These mistaken associations, this confusion of causality and coincidence, will lead us into the irrationality of superstition.

A shaman is one who tricks the gods, nothing more. She or he, by observing repetition, claims knowledge of the deeper workings of the world, and uses trickery to try to modify future events. While everyone else is out hunting and gathering, the shaman tries to influence those activities by playing tricks on the supreme powers. To this end, rituals, formulae lacking all semantic meaning, and previously non-existent symbols are created – a repertoire that the shaman tries to hide, in order to maintain their superior status in the group. When the shaman tries to heal a hunter's wound, she or he might happen upon a plant with beneficial properties, but a dozen other factors that actually make no difference will also – by coincidence – come into play. The same will be the case with the superstitious person who decides to repeat a certain set of circumstances only because they coincide with a lucky event.

And so human beings tried to deceive the natural world, projecting imaginary forces onto its workings and, to that end, cooking up certain artificial tricks. And thereby ended up caught in a net of their own delusional making.

Unfortunately, our thinking is something that creates mirrors. And not good mirrors, either.

Later on, when we human beings come to leave behind our tribes and the nomadic way of life, and the small gatherings of huts begin to transform into cities, the aspiration to control the unfolding of events will prove insufficient. And we will embark on a new, more ambitious enterprise: a search for meaning that explains our existence.

Magical thinking will come to work side by side with another of our mind's excrescences: mythical thinking. Which, little by little, will gradually displace it in the majority of spaces.

This half-built world still lacks order and meaning. Which is why the primitive mind of humans needs to come up with a context to explain and protect itself, a narrative that gives significance to its presence in a world as yet unfurnished with conceptual layers and abstract trappings. The myth will imply, as a consequence, a narrator and a number of listeners possessed of intelligence. And a ritual, too, which, unlike magic, will not be occult but entirely social, with the asemantic formulae being replaced by signification. Men and women start inventing stories: tales told around the fire once their hunger is sated, as entertainment; legends, with extraordinary historical events recreated as a way of aiding group cohesion; and myths, when the narration is considered sacred and accompanied by liturgical rites.

The creator of the myth does not see her- or himself as inventing a fiction. Not all con artists know themselves to be liars. Rather, they feel they have been chosen by the gods, and believe that the unfiltered truth is being revealed to them through inspiration. They have discerned life's meaninglessness, and because of this concoct a story in which justice is the ruling principle, making up for the incomprehensible injustice that causes all the desolation they see in the world around them. For this, they see no option but to divide the world in two: with the world of the mortals, inhabited in ordinary time; and that of the gods and of myth, where a primordial time reigns – a past that never passed because it is so utterly replete with meaning – such that the gods may always be there.

Thus, when human beings stop having to worry about survival, they start reflecting on existence. Magic moves into the background and their speculative intelligence begins forging inventions that are more complex still.

And then we get the founding of religions.

GOD THE DECEIVER

Human beings spread across the planet and continue in their tireless construction of the world.

They look at the forests and invent sacred trees. In Nordic myth, Odin describes the cosmos as a giant ash tree containing the nine worlds. The same in the Hindu Upanishads, which also feature a cosmic tree, this time turned upside down as a representation of the universe burying its roots in the sky and spreading its branches over the land. In the times of the Buddha, sacred places with stones, water and trees representing a microcosm were omnipresent, and neither Buddhism nor Hinduism would fully succeed in wresting their religious value from them. From the Indus Valley to Egypt, trees will be an endlessly fertile cosmic source, seen as the incarnations of huge naked goddesses. In Mesopotamian culture, these trees have sacred powers by virtue of being vertical, because they grow and because, though they lose their leaves, they will always come back into leaf again. In Greece, from Minoan times to the end of Hellenism, places of worship always featured a tree beside a rock, and in Judaism the tree, or *Asherah*, is present as part of the altar. As essential manifestations of the cosmos, rhizomes, shrubs and lotus flowers will all be assigned symbolic power.

And wherever these humans with their imperfect intelligence look, the same thing happens.

If they contemplate a rock, they immediately feel its hardness and durability to be a divine manifestation. And they apply themselves to the laborious assembly of funerary megaliths, fertility monoliths, dolmens and menhirs. In the ancient tribes of India, stones up to 3 metres tall would be placed alongside tombs as a way of anchoring the dead soul and providing it with a place to shelter in the vicinity of the living. And newlyweds would go and ask the megaliths to give them children. In the Australian interior, where people believe that their ancestors inhabit dolmens and have the power to bestow fertility, there is a custom of barren women going and rubbing their bodies against the stone. In the native Maidu people of California, as well, they go and rub against a stone in the shape of a pregnant woman. And, in both Madagascar and the Kai Islands, such fertility stones are also daubed with lubricating fats.

Should these most advanced of primates then come across a stretch of water, they cannot help but think of it as the source of all things, of all existence – as held by the Vedic tradition. And ideas about its purifying power will come to mind. And thoughts of baptism. Ablutions. The biblical flood. And they will create gods like the Nordic Aegir, or the Greek Poseidon – traditions also overflowing with other, lesser divinities like the nymphs, who are the goddesses of running water, fountains and springs. And there will be all sorts of European peoples who, like the Cimbri, the Franks, the Germans and the Slavs, will go to their rivers to offer sacrifice.

In short, human beings seem incapable of looking at anything without producing ghosts. Whether looking down at the ground or raising their eyes to the sky, they hatch vast telluric or celestial epiphanies. The Maoris speak of a goddess of the earth and a god of the sky – Papa and Rangi – that are locked in an eternal embrace and give birth to innumerable children. In the African tribes, too, there are primordial earth–sky couples: Oduna and Olorum in the Yoruba, Ewe and Akwapim traditions; and Nzambi-Mpungu and Nzambi for the Bawili. In southern California, Mother Earth is Tamaiovit and Father Sky is Tukmit, and, for the Navajo people, the wife is Naestsan and her celestial husband Yadilyil. In Greek myth, the first thing engendered by Gaia is a creature who is her equal, one who can cover her over: Uranus, or the starry sky. The same sky that would later transform into the supreme deity of the Hebrews, the wrathful Old Testament Yahweh, who evolves from the early celestial and atmospheric hierophants to manifest in storms, with His thunderous voice, the arrows of His thunderbolts, His fire and floods.

The zeal of the fantasist hominid knows no end: the sky itself contains other elements capable of being reinterpreted, and the stars will be turned into signs of the Zodiac; from Neolithic times, it will attribute the moon with power over cosmic phenomena, over agriculture, the rains, the fertility of women and animals, rites of passage and death. The sun will be personified as so many other gods, and in Egyptian mythology alone inspire the creation of divinities such as Horus, Atum, Jepri, Jnum, Ra, Amon-Ra and Aton. But when this hominid tries to get its feet on the ground and concentrate on the soil and its labours, still it won't be able to avoid trying to improve its crops with the most foolish practices. In Estonia, the men will go out to sow the fields naked in the middle of the night, while during droughts in India women will strip naked to pull the plough through the fields. German peasants will pour water over themselves to ensure a good crop, based on an inferred resemblance between the rain and seminal fluid. In Finland, women pour breast milk into the field furrows. The Aztecs made offerings to the first corn that sprouted, and treated it as though it were divine; three months after germination, they would decapitate a young woman in front of it as well, as a representation of the goddess of the new corn, Chicomecóatl; two months later, they would also sacrifice another woman, who represented the goddess of the gathered corn, Toci. Certain native peoples of America, as with certain African tribes, dismember the young woman and bury her body parts in the furrows. In Bengal, the females who were offered up had in turn to be the daughters of previously sacrificed women, who from birth were destined to burn on the pyre – though they did live well for a time on the parcel of land they were afforded, and were permitted to marry other martyrs. Agricultural sacrifices were also carried out in Egypt, Syria and Mesopotamia, and vestiges of such practices are present in Germany, Sweden, Poland and Greece. In the Bible, to multiply Abraham's offspring and bless his seed, God says: 'Take now thy son, thine only son Isaac, whom thou lovest, and get thee into the land of Moriah; and offer him there for a burnt offering upon one of the mountains which I will tell thee of' (Genesis, 22:2).

All of which has meant that, in scarcely a millennium or two, humans have succeeded in filling the world to the brim with previously non-existent phantasmagoria and figments of the imagination, in a bloody process that has taken in mass torture, murder, persecution, holy wars and genocide.

The only practical difference between religion and superstition – both of which issue out of mistaken ideas about causality and the same chimerical imagination – is that the former is more organized. Religion seeks to *religare* – Latin for 'bind': to group together and reunite the variety of acquired beliefs and cult practices, to form a single corpus. It aspires to become something larger and longer-lasting, and above all to ensure its grip on power. All its liturgical rites have to be carried out in strict accordance with its rules, which over time will themselves become more precise, coercive and sophisticated. They will also multiply in number, thereby assuring them of a uniqueness in the face of their adversaries.

And it is quite the paradox, considering that we are talking about two virtually identical sisters, that one should begin to persecute the other with such vigour and viciousness. The moment religion felt sufficiently strong and secure, it declared war on superstition, on the unbelievers – that is, anybody who did not believe in its entelechies. And in this war, no quarter was given. In Exodus, we see commands such as, 'Thou shalt not suffer a witch to live', and in Leviticus: 'And the soul that turneth after such as have familiar spirits, and after wizards, to go a-whoring after them, I will even set my face against that soul, and will cut him off from among his people.' The struggle for power became increasingly bitter, and the more bellicose and well organized of the sisters had everything to fight for. Within the framework of religions themselves, it will be the monotheistic ones that expand more efficiently than the polytheistic, not because any of them is truer – truth being a concept made up entirely as we go along – nor because any of the stories they offer make them preferable. Rather, it is because a plurality of gods disperses people's fervour and promotes greater levels of tolerance, while a single, exclusive deity feeds and fuels fanaticism.

Christianity has made it clear from the beginning, when the precedents of the platonic doctrine, Judaism and the Egyptian god Aton, under the auspices of the pharaoh Akhenaton, led it to become the principal monotheism in the Mediterranean: thou shalt have no other God but me.

Thus, Christianity managed to impose its dogma across the western hemisphere, introducing countless novel lies into our culture: the concept of sin, the idea of guilt, and so many others that are so familiar that we can barely differentiate between them and our own thoughts, such as the idea of expiation, eternal damnation and resurrection; it also ushered in a particular idea of goodness, which has made us think that we are not able to be independently good but have to be God-fearing and bent on the egoistic goal of seeking our own salvation; misogyny, homophobia, sexual repression; a simplistic sort of heaven only vaguely described, and a far more detailed, terrifying hell; and, as the backdrop, the idea of the soul as immortal.

From the moment when human beings are in possession of this fictional personal identity, the fear of then losing it will even outstrip the survival instinct. And if there is a primordial time inhabited by the gods, why should humans not hope for their precious identity to be conserved forever in that same eternal place? That first illusion only needed an added pinch of transcendence to become something far more elevated – the soul – which then gets to go to the glorifying party as well and have a bit of sacred cake. The Christian faith, unlike what happens with the principal eastern religions – whose ultimate goal is the dissolution of the illusory ego in order to break the cycle of reincarnation – has been one of the greatest promoters of individuality. So that it can present itself as the one true consolation for this atavistic fear, and in order to keep its believers in submission with the promise of extreme rewards or punishments – eternal ones – Christianity declared, with neither proof nor justification, that the soul was immortal.

By the sixteenth century – or 1516, to be precise – two different works were published offering sober objections to the everlastingness of souls. On the one hand, you have the *Treatise on the Immortality of Souls* by Italian philosopher Pietro Pomponazzi, and, on the other, Thomas More's *Utopia*. Unlike Pomponazzi, More was never considered an atheist, and even went on to be canonized by the Catholic Church. Yet neither of the two could find any rational argument in favour of this kind of immortality. That is, from a place of pure reason, there was no way to demonstrate anything but our corruptibility, and one had to fall back on faith and Revelation to find support for these beliefs. I would also like to recommend here a delicious diatribe by David Hume that was published in 1777 – posthumously, that is, at Hume's behest, and more than twenty years after it was written. In 'On the Immortality of the Soul', the Scottish philosopher definitively unmasked the fallacy of immortality, and all of his arguments – specifically the physical ones, which for Hume were the building blocks of knowledge – have gone on to be endorsed by neurology. For the precursor of contemporary empiricism, there are clear correlations between body and soul in infancy, in the full health of adulthood and in the decline of old age, from which it is only possible to deduce that the following step is as predictable as it is inevitable: the dissolution of the soul after death. Over time, the medical literature on physical trauma, mental illnesses and studies carried out on the brain has come to show that the mind, the identity and the so-called soul are as unstable as they are ephemeral. We now know that, if we make an intervention in this or that part of the brain, we can erase old memories or alter the capacity for short-term memory, as well as potentially compromising speech and causing a wide range of aphasias. Studies have been carried out on the effect of degenerative illness not only on memory, awareness or speech, but every single other aspect of a patient's identity or personality. This opens the way to no end of awkward questions. Will somebody suffering a childhood ailment that has mental repercussions meaning they never develop an adult personality continue being that same arrested child when they are beyond the grave, or will God save the adult they never became?

We could examine, one by one, all the pieces of evidence against the existence of an immortal soul. But perhaps at the stage we find ourselves in history, the point has already been made, and there is little sense going on when we have just mentioned the most complex idea of the many to have arisen out of magical and mythical thinking, out of our psychological weakness – the idea of God.

If there is something that Christianity constantly turns to when it can find no other way to demonstrate its remaining articles of faith, it is the idea of God, the supreme imaginary being and apogee of all the phantasmagorical material brought forth by the mind of humans: the first illusion, sustaining the metaphysical condition of all the other ones. An all-powerful and omni-benevolent God who allows for the existence of evil in the world; who can forgive, but not for all of eternity; and who in the Old Testament gives ample evidence of His cruel, merciless, jealous and vengeful nature, and who in the New Testament will also send a son to earth who will show himself all too frequently as violent, capricious, despotic and verbose. An all-powerful and omni-benevolent God who creates a human being full of defects and limitations, with cognitive faculties so stunted that they allow only a poor sense of things – never direct knowledge of them – but of whom at the same time absolute faith in His unproven existence is demanded. A self-sufficient, perfect God who needs nothing, and yet, in a rare show of immeasurable egoism, needs constant reverence and devotion from us. A God who, though nothing is beyond Him, has not seen fit to return among us, except for in the distant past of the illiterate tribes who wandered the desert beset on all sides by hunger, ignorance and magical thinking. A God from whom truth itself issues, whose word is the Truth (John, 17:17) and who is called the God of Truth (Isaiah, 65:16), and who, nonetheless, when He came to create the best of all possible worlds, made it on the basis of appearances, filled it with mistaken intuitions and deceptions and has ensured that everything, plants and animals included – even long before the emergence of humans, the peerless fabricators – was moved by a throughgoing inclination to lie.

Over time, all the rational arguments in favour of the existence of God have been refuted by reason itself. Some are so fallacious that it takes barely any effort to swat them aside – for example, the so-called 'historical argument', the 'proof of tradition' and the 'proof of universal consent', the last of these justifying that existence by the fact that all the peoples on earth have at some point believed in (a) god. Others, such as Saint Anselm's argument – which, as we have seen, Descartes fell back on in order to escape the trap of solipsism – have been negated from the bosom of Scholasticism itself. For Anselm of Canterbury, we are capable of conceiving of infinity, but this infinity or God would be even greater and more perfect if it really existed and not only inside our minds; therefore, the infinite must exist. And there you have it, proof of God. Thomas Aquinas himself will question Saint Anselm, pointing out that people will interpret God only as the greatest thing that may be thought. But, even letting this premise stand, he will point out that such reasoning implies only an ideal existence, not a real one. Immanuel Kant, who dubbed Anselmian reasoning as the 'ontological argument', will maintain that the a priori demonstration of God could only be seen as a postulation of practical reason – that is, a question of faith. And, just like Kant, many others will negate the possibility of scientifically demonstrating God's existence. Karl Popper is one for whom there is no way to disprove God's existence, because, as with ghosts or any other fantastical invention, it isn't possible to refute the statement 'God exists' with a concrete empirical rebuttal.

Even the strongest arguments for God's existence, such as the 'teleological argument' – which is Aristotelian in origin and coincides with Saint Thomas's fifth way – have been amply debunked. This line of reasoning points to the world's seeming purpose, to the fact it is too well ordered and complex to have arisen out of sheer chance, and that it must therefore have been created by some intelligent being, which is what we call God. Nonetheless, this logic – should anyone choose to deploy it in this day and age – intentionally conceals the huge role played by chance in the formation of the universe and in the unfolding of life. The cosmos has had millions of years to carry out each of its movements – it wasn't made in six days at the behest of some demiurge, but uses vast lapses of time in order for certain random coincidences and circumstances to come together. Evolution itself also works without any pre-planned intentions, by trial and error, and, as every biologist knows, the missteps far outweigh the correct moves. David Hume, who anticipated this objection, even got in ahead of the idea of natural selection: could an animal that wasn't correctly put together possibly survive? Only the best-adapted animals survive. Even the world itself wouldn't go on if it weren't properly arranged. And why could such apparent order not be the work of unintelligent agents whose actions happen to appear vaguely anthropic? The teleological argument would only lead us to wonder which intelligent creator made the mind of God, which is also well organized – and so on, ad infinitum.

The existence of God, in short – as would be the case with the immortality of the soul – can be proved neither by empirical experience, nor by scientific method, nor on the basis of reasoning argument. The only hope lies in miracles. But in any case, we have to admit, it has been quite a while since miracles stopped appearing. For some strange reason, they only appeared in dark times and places in which humans were steeped in ignorance.

And at this point we can only turn to the conclusions Ludwig Feuerbach comes to in *The Essence of Christianity*: God did not create man in his image and likeness, but, rather, it was man who, by using his imagination and projecting his own qualities, created God. In the first place, man formed an image of God based on what he himself was like – that is, by transforming his own abstract intellectual essence into a fantastical being. And, after that, he conferred this entity with a real existence in the outside world. The essence of God is therefore the objectified essence of fantasy, the representation of all human desires, hopes and dreams.

Religion, Feuerbach will say, thus constructed an anthropic divinity as a consequence of man's self-love and as a means for self-affirmation. Hence the fact that every religion will hold the gods of every other religion as nothing more than misconceptions. And the Christian religion, in particular, will end up encouraging a schism inside man, in that it considers God a being that is opposed to him. For Christianity, God is all that man is, but in infinitely greater measure: if God is the infinite being, man is by necessity the finite being; if God is perfect, man is imperfect; if God is eternal, man is ephemeral; if God is omnipotent, man is important; if God is holy, man is culpable and sinful. The lie that is God and the being that is man will be defined as two conflicting poles, where the former represents that which is absolutely positive, the content of all realities, and the latter, by distinction, only the negative, the closest thing to nothingness.

Hence why it is so necessary for us to discover that the real secret behind theology is anthropology. The decisive turn in history will come about at the moment when man understands that the consciousness of God is nothing but the consciousness of the species.

If it were not for this, we would go on being deceived – self-deceived, properly speaking – by an external God who is just a projection of ourselves.

We can take this position or we can fall back on faith. There is no way to prevent anyone from believing in God on the basis of faith.

Through faith, of course, God's existence can be justified.

As can anything else.

THE LIES OF THE CHURCH

Any person is free to believe whatever they want on the basis of faith.

It would be desirable, though, for the believer who, as well as believing, wishes to opine – and even impose their opinion on others – to submit to a deep purging of their real beliefs and to become familiar with the basic notions of the history and sociology of religion. Because the idea that all opinions are equal is a lie.

It is common nowadays to hear people say they are Christian while at the same time – out of intellectual laziness, which would not be at all to their God's liking – giving no thought to what it is they really believe. If the main body of the Christian church who don't go to mass were asked why they are non-practising, there is a standard and fairly recurrent answer: 'I believe in God, but I don't believe in the church.'

The answer seems reasonable to me, in a way. After all, their God is everywhere, and in the holy scriptures the divine desire for a church to be erected in His name barely gets a mention beyond a single line mentioning a rock (Matthew, 16:18), whereas express bans on the professionalization of the priesthood get plenty of mentions (Hebrews, 7:21–5). Nonetheless, given that the church, through the various councils, has constructed and transformed the concept of

God and the principal articles of faith over the course of history, it seems reasonable to ask: exactly what God does the Christian believe in who believes in God but not the church? A believer of this kind would need to refine and define their beliefs as soon as possible, because how can they be sure of worshipping the true God if their faith is directed only towards a church that has never done anything but lie?

The struggle for power and control over God's revealed truth is as old as Christianity itself. In the first and second centuries of our era, it was the church that decided which among more than fifty gospels and other documents concerning the figure of Jesus of Nazareth were and were not valid. Why the choice of the four canonical gospels and none of the others, such as the gospel of Mary Magdalene or the gospel of Judas? Doubtless it was just a question of internal disputes and rivalries, given that these texts were all contemporary, arising out of the various schools of thought and sects that sprang up in the Mediterranean at that time. It all depended on who got in first or who best established their mechanisms of power. If Irenaeus, Bishop of Lyon, hadn't managed to overcome the Gnostic movement, and the gospel of Judas had succeeded in joining the canon, current-day Christian dogma would be a different thing altogether.[1]

[1] Not only would we have an entirely favourable vision of Judas Iscariot, as Jesus' favourite disciple and an enabler of his sacrifice, but the crucifixion and resurrection would never so much as have been mentioned, and the now frowned-upon Gnostic principles would have triumphed: in Gnosticism, the creator of this world is neither the greatest god nor a divinity we ought to worship, but merely the last in a long line of self-begetting deities – the weakest and most defective of all, and one we would do well to turn away from.

Moreover, nobody should overlook how widespread and constant the doubts are over the historicity of the accounts in the canonical gospels. There are many reasons for these suspicions, but a number of them are quite fundamental. To begin with, these texts were written a century after the death of Jesus, which would mean that their authors could not have been direct witnesses to the life of Christianity's central figure: Papyrus P52, also known as the St John's fragment, is the oldest New Testament manuscript we have, and the experts date it between the years 125 and 160. Second, the four canonical gospels were written in Greek, and not in Aramaic, which was the language Jesus spoke – though he didn't know how to write – and the language of his disciples. Third, in spite of the remarkable similarities of style between the three Synoptic gospels (Matthew, Mark, Luke), there are discrepancies between the successive biographies of which they claim to consist, certain contradictions that become even greater when compared with the gospel of John, and which would be completely impossible to tally if the entirety of the so-called apocryphal gospels were taken into account. These three issues point to the fact that the true authors of these books were anonymous individuals who took pieces of information from the sayings of Jesus, which were much discussed in their time, gave them a narrative shape and then attributed them to the main players in the life of the subject, or to others who enjoyed prestige within their communities. And yet, in spite of the absolute rational and scientific impossibility of the four canonical gospels having been written by the apostles, what is the church's official line when presented with this evidence? It lies. In our present day, the church still clings to the same position as ever, apparently regardless of all that has gone on around it:

> The Church has always argued, and continues to argue, that the four gospels are apostolic in origin. For that which the Apostles had Christ's mandate to preach, and then with the Holy Spirit as their inspiration, they and the Apostolic Men transmitted to us in writing, founding the faith, that is, the Gospel in four parts, according to Matthew, Mark, Luke and John. (II Vatican Council, 25 January 1959)

Which means that, long before the church even began any substantial transformation of the Christian dogma in its various ecumenical councils, its own origins – like just about everything when it comes to humanity – were forged in internal rivalries, fraud and falsehood. The facts of Jesus' life, as much as the principles and values that have gone on to spread beyond Christian doctrine, could just as easily have been different.

Nevertheless, I am not going to question the historical existence of Jesus of Nazareth. I will take as given that he lived and breathed – in spite of the scarcity of documents from his own time; in spite of the fact that none of the writers active in the cities through which he passed makes any mention of his miracles; in spite of the fact that every reference to his life comes exclusively from religious texts a century later and none of the ones dated before the gospels provides a single biographical detail.[2] I am going to suppose that a person with this name did walk the earth, a

[2] Before the gospels, there was a whole century with no historical trace whatsoever of Jesus. Not even in the epistles of Saint Paul, who was a contemporary of Jesus, can any information be found about his life as a real person. On the contrary, every time Paul alludes to his Messiah, he speaks of him as though he had lived in a primordial time, essentially separated from his own; and when he does, he carefully cleaves to the archetype of the mythical hero.

person in whom biographical features of other personalities of the time could just have happened to converge, and around whom different doctrines present in the Middle East just happened to come together. I will admit that he is a historical possibility – though there is a growing number of experts who put the idea in doubt[3] – given the difficulty involved in demonstrating the non-existence of a person from the past. That is, only because it is impossible to refute strictly existential statements; in the words of Karl Popper, we cannot register the totality of the world with the aim of determining that something did not exist, never existed and will never exist.

---

[3] A brief list of the historians, theologians and specialists from around the world who question Jesus' historicity would include Prosper Alfaric, John M. Allegro, Joseph Atwill, Héctor Ávalos, Nigel Barber, Bruno Bauer, Charles Bradlaugh, Thomas L. Brodie, Francesco Carotta, Steven Carr, Richard Carrier, Luigi Cascioli, Hal Childs, Greta Christina, Paul-Louis Couchoud, Gary Courtney, Jerry Coyne, Philip R. Davies, Richard Dawkins, Herman Detering, Earl Doherty, Arthur Drews, Arthur Droge, Charles-François Dupuis, Maria Dzielska, Lena Einhorn, Alvar Ellegård, David Fitzgerald, Timothy Freke, Robert W. Funk, Peter Gandy, Neil Godfrey, Phyllis Graham, Tom Harpur, Fritz Heede, Godfrey Higgins, Christopher Hitchens, R. Joseph Hoffmann, Paul Hopper, Stephan Huller, Kenneth Humphreys, John G. Jackson, Peter Jensen, Michael Kalopoulos, Peter Kirby, Abner Kneeland, Alvin Boyd Kuhn, Georges Las Vergnas, Raphael Lataster, Harold Leidner, Samuel Lublinski, Gerd Lüdemann, Dennis MacDonald, Burton Mack, Michael Martin, Gerald Massey, Joseph McCabe, Harita Meenee, Christos Morfos, Ioannis Mpousios, D. M. Murdock, Derek Murphy, Payam Nabarz, Kurt Noll, Michel Onfray, Georges Ory, Clarke W. Owens, Thomas Paine, Minas Papageorgiou, Michael B. Paulkovich, Steven Pinker, Robert M. Price, Jay Raskin, Salomon Reinach, Samuel Max Rieser, John Mackinnon Robertson, Loren Rosson, René Salm, Gunnar Samuelsson, David Oliver Smith, Rudolf Steck, Gordon Stein, Valerie Tarico, Thomas L. Thompson, Pier Tulip, Michael Turton, Daniel Unterbrink, Edward van der Kaaij, Raoul Vaneigem, Thomas S. Verenna, Nikos Vergidis, Roger Viklund, Barbara Walker, George Albert Wells and Frank Zindler.

I will instead take issue with the cornerstone on which the whole of Christianity is built, the most central of all the lies cooked up by the Catholic Church: nothing less than Jesus Christ's crucifixion and resurrection.

Though still not that widely known in society, among scholars, translators and exegetes of the scriptures there is an acceptance that there were never two defendants in Jesus' supposed trial before Pontius Pilate. The story that has come down to us first started being altered several decades later, when the new Christian community had begun distancing itself from the Jewish community. But it is clear that, before these modifications, Jesus and Barabbas were one and the same character. We now know that Barabbas is a Greek rendering of the Aramaic Bar'-Abbā', which means 'son of the Father', and is etymologically linked to bar-Rabbam, or 'son of our Master'. Both converge on a single sobriquet, 'master', which was how Christ's followers referred to him. Curiously enough, Barabbas' first name was also Yeshua, or Jesus; another fact that the ecclesiastical authorities have tried their hardest to hide, so that it has now disappeared from its original place – Matthew, 27:16 – in eight out of ten translations of the original manuscript. This Jesus the Master, according to the gospels, had been thrown in jail for taking part in a riot, and was indeed famous among the Jews, having been accused of sedition against the Roman Empire. This once again coincides with the principal biographies of Jesus Christ. When Pontius Pilate, procurator of the Roman province of Judaea, asked the people gathered which prisoner he ought to set free for the Hebrew Passover celebrations, the crowd that had amassed around their leader shouted out: 'Jesus the Master! Jesus Barabbas! Jesus the Christ!'

We cannot forget that this was the same crowd that a little while earlier had acclaimed Jesus on his entrance into the city, and was made up in large part of his followers and supporters.

This changes everything.

To begin with, it wasn't the human species in its entirety that so despicably betrayed Jesus Christ. This in part reduces the magnitude of his sacrifice, but above all is a huge mitigation of the burden of guilt we have borne ever since.

On the other hand, this manipulation of the scriptures by the first Christians, planned when hostilities between them and the remaining Jewish communities were on the increase, had more than just short-term results. Unfortunately, by turning Jesus into two characters and dramatizing the betrayal by the people of Israel, they created a very negative image of the Hebrews of the time, which ended up giving rise to the main historical antisemitic allegation and aroused such hate that it has brought Jews to the brink of genocide on numerous occasions. This once more shows that a well-wrought fiction is always stronger than any rationally made argument.

If Pontius Pilate had actually ended up accommodating the Jewish custom of freeing a prisoner at Passover, ceding to the wish of the people, that would be the end of the story. Jesus of Nazareth would have walked out of Jerusalem a free man, and the miracle of the resurrection would never have taken place. And that would have been that. Nonetheless, had Pilate observed the Roman laws and customs, and at the last moment sent Christ to the cross, specialists on the subject point to other, far more plausible theories than that of a real historical person subsequently rising from the dead. That is, following Hume's probability criterion, any of these theories would be more acceptable than a phenomenon that none of us – hand on heart – would believe if we heard it today without all the cultural baggage attached.

We cannot in the end avoid the possibility of syncretism and the fact that the concept of resurrection was well established in all the traditions of this region: Osiris came back to life in Egypt, Baal did so in Canaan, as did Attis in Greek mythology, the Phoenician and Syrian god Adonis and the Semitic Tammuz, and the miracle of rising from the dead was absolutely the most commonplace prophecy among the many in the lands of Israel.

According to one theory, the body of Christ could have been removed from his grave by a disciple. This possibility was included in the New Testament itself, in an attempt to cover its back against inevitable misgivings: 'Say ye, His disciples came by night, and stole him away while we slept . . . So they took the money, and did as they were taught: and this saying is commonly reported among the Jews until this day' (Matthew, 28:13–15). And, indeed, insinuations of this kind carried on for centuries. Had this been the case, had Christ's body been taken from his sepulchre by his disciples, it could have been with the best of intentions – they could have been convinced of his imminent resurrection and therefore wanted their Messiah to be with them when he returned. Then again, given that his cortège was made up of as many as seventy followers, there is also the possibility that some of them carried out the plan premeditatedly, in which case what we have here is the greatest instance of fraud and marketing in the history of all religions.

Another theory centres on the figure of Caiaphas, who had motivation in wishing to conserve his power as the most senior religious representative among the Jews, and could have made the body disappear in order that he could then tell his adepts to go looking for it in Galilee, thereby avoiding Jesus' tomb becoming a site of pilgrimage that would mean the legend growing. Evidently, he would have miscalculated the effects of such a disappearance.

And there are many other hypotheses besides, looking into the frequency of the sacking of tombs in Judaea at that time, the demand for vital organs of both the recently deceased and holy figures for use in the most widely practised rituals, and making it clear that the condemned would get dumped in mass graves in those days, as well as how common it was for burial places to get mixed up – all eventualities more plausible than a miracle.

And, even so, what does an empty grave prove? Certainly, the image of the unoccupied niche was very widespread as a symbol among the Hebrew sects, and among these resurrection was something that also featured relatively frequently. But when a body disappears from a grave or morgue nowadays, our first thought is to call the police – the last thing we think is that the body has risen from the dead. Or, in other words, if this was going to be the central and most extraordinary miracle in all Christianity, would Jesus have not spent a little longer among the living after coming back to life? Could he not have let more witnesses see him, gone walking around among the crowds, let himself be carried shoulder high before Caiaphas and the rest of his enemies? Because what sense is there in coming back to life only to ascend to heaven immediately afterwards? We should not forget that Christ, for the church, since it was approved in 381 at the Council of Nicaea, is consubstantial with God. He would therefore have known all that the future contained, had mastery of the most complex scientific disciplines in the future, been able to speak every language, even known how to write, but if, for some unfathomable reason, he had decided to leave no other evidence of his divinity than the resurrection, could he not at least have done so in a way that left the matter beyond all doubt?

Compared with the invention of this trick, what difference do the rest of the church's lies make? What could it matter that none of the disciples ever notices Mary's virginity, something that goes completely unremarked by them for decades, or that the only support for this striking miracle lies in a single translation error from the Old Testament (Isaiah 7:14)? Another calculated slip by the translators of the original – the substitution of the word 'young woman' or 'damsel' with 'virgin', in a single instance – that the Catholic Church continues to hide to this day. Or has it perhaps bothered any of those who have gone on talking up her virginity during all this time that Mary should have had four more boys and as many girls with Joseph (Matthew 13:54–8; Mark, 6:1–6; Luke, 8:19–21; John, 2:12)? Once we accept the miracle of the resurrection and give way to credulousness, all the other anomalies become mere details. What does it matter that Jesus did not ask for a church to be founded in his name, or that he explicitly prohibited priesthood becoming a profession because it would set some men above others? Who, in short, has seen it as an obstacle that the Bible roundly states that 'God that made the world and all things therein, seeing that he is Lord of heaven and earth, dwelleth not in temples made with hands' (Acts, 17:24), or that it so clearly admonished the worship of images?

> For the customs of the people are vain: for one cutteth a tree out of the forest, the work of the hands of the work-

> man, with the axe. They deck it with silver and with gold; they fasten it with nails and with hammers, that it move not. They are upright as the palm tree, but speak not: they must needs be borne, because they cannot go. Be not afraid of them; for they cannot do evil, neither also is it in them to do good.

Idols, which fill modern-day Catholic churches to overflowing, and which even fill the streets for at least one week a year, could not resemble more closely that which the revealed texts repudiate. But let's not forget that Christian iconography itself often represents fate with a bandage over her eyes.

Only from this perspective is it possible to explain the triumph of a church – the Vatican – that said 'Thou shalt not covet' and yet surrounded itself with jewels and wealth and luxury, accumulating riches in previously unimaginable ways.

It said: 'Thou shalt not kill.' And unleashed the Crusades and the Inquisition, the greatest mechanisms for torture and genocide created by humanity until the Nazis came along with the Final Solution.

And it said: 'Thou shalt not lie.' And invented the Truth.

THE LIES OF ATHEISM

But let's not fool ourselves.

The atheist who says God does not exist also lies.

It is true that in a Popperian sense we can posit His non-existence as a scientific hypothesis, because it is highly falsifiable: we would need no more than an empirical intuition of God in order for it to be negated. But it is nothing more than this, a hypothesis – a conjecture that could be of use to us for only a moment. It is also true that we have found not a single argument to justify God's existence, whereas we have arrived at an array of theories that would make a divine explanation redundant. Nonetheless, beyond this, we know absolutely nothing about what is out there. We can't know. There could be anything at all lying in wait on the other side, and, to our limited cognitive abilities, it could assume the most unexpected and inconceivable form. In this sense, the atheist's every pretension to absolute certainty is nothing more than a further imposture. A question of faith, again.

Should the atheist declare that God does not exist, they would be lying, just as the sceptic would be if they try to claim that other people don't exist. These are, however, two different categories of lie.

In the case of the latter – although, from a purely logical point of view, I have no irrefutable argument at my disposal that would allow me to declare that other people's minds do not exist – it is a hypothesis at least continuously refuted by the senses. Time and again, our empirical impressions tell us that other people are indeed there. With God, you don't even get that.

It would therefore be worth distinguishing – as a way in, although we will come back to this at a later stage – between two large groups of presumptions. The idea of God would be placed in the first, alongside all the other chimeras, in a situation similar to that of unicorns, angels, the Gorgons, the Leviathan, the Loch Ness monster, Atlantis, Lilliput, Neverland, Tlön and the immortality of the soul. Though they all obviously form part of our culture, the fact they have been scientifically disproven means there is a provisionality to them; they are still awaiting positive verification. Meanwhile, and by contrast, a second group would include the hypotheses of non-existence that have already been refuted, at least empirically, such as the law of gravity and the existence of other people.

This is not to say that we can consider the second group as truths, and far less as certainties on a par with 'cogito ergo sum.' They are all equally fictions of our own conceiving.

Scientific hypotheses are, however, more *plausible* lies.

And, in essence, the lies for which we have sense-based, direct and continuous evidence – from what our eyes, ears and skin tell us – are far more difficult to disbelieve.

THE FORMATION OF SOCIETIES

In a world or universe in which the lie has proved to be an agent for regulation as well as something that reaps benefits, human beings stand out over all other species as having the greatest capacity for generating fictions. This adeptness for trickery has led them to subjugate all the other living beings on earth, leading to a mastery – albeit transient, and more based on impulse than on reason – of their environment.

But, kind reader, let us go back to the naked ape.

We have already covered at least two aspects of lying that led to this supremacy of humans. On the one hand, by beginning to make use of the rudiments of deception, practical applications were brought into play, along with language and knowledge of a certain kind. On the other, the ability to tell stories aided the cohesion and organization of larger groups. One, two: knowledge and cohesion. Nonetheless, lying had a third property that was just as necessary as these two – if not more so – in the formation of societies. It was only the ability to lie to one another – and even to ourselves – on a constant basis that made such an association tolerable; otherwise, we would never have put up with being lumped together with strangers. So, there is number three: co-existence.

As we have also said, we need fiction in order to reach the barest unity of knowledge. Long before the first advanced hominids learned to talk and to tell stories around the fire, they had already required lies in order to develop symbolic thought. To set the process of abstraction in motion, the first thing the mind needs is metaphor: a mechanism that, through substitution, allows for the creation of comprehensive images of the world. So, the first metaphoric leap comes when the nervous impulse produced by our senses is transformed into a mental image. Making metaphor the memory of a smell or the mental representation of a loved one, just as it will later be a bison sketched on a rock face. Metaphor will be the abstraction of any chain of events, even those that have not yet taken place. Metaphor, substitution and speculative falsification are the only things that will enable us to remember and predict, and to repeat the procedure by which we succeeded in kindling fire, or anticipate the movements of predators or prey. A couple of million years later, the second metaphoric leap takes place when image is transformed into sound. This gives rise to concepts and language. We therefore cannot deny that metaphor undergirds every process to do with knowledge and understanding. It is the linguistic nucleus that enables us both to make sense of the world and to design other possible worlds. Any discussion of metaphor, as Umberto Eco would say, at the very minimum also means discussing symbols, ideograms, models, archetypes, dreams, desires, delirium, ritual, myth, magic, creativity, paradigms, icons and representation, as well as being the only thing that makes it possible to have language itself, and signs, and sense, and meaning. The building blocks of understanding lie in poeticizing. There is no alternative; human intelligence knows no other way. All of our knowledge, therefore, is based on speculation, projection and lies. And all of contemporary science – its self-appointment on the altar of truth, formerly occupied by religion – not only has these same poetic mechanisms as its basis, inasmuch as it is elaborated by individuals, but, in order to advance, also has to build upon paradigms – that is, on untested sets of theories, transitory postulations and hypotheses that are no less fictional in nature.

Once symbolic knowledge has given rise to language, what will set *Homo sapiens* apart from all other members of the *Homo* genus won't be inventions or clever gadgets, but its capacity for cohesion. First, thanks to language, the small groups of hominids will be able to organize and come up with hunting strategies – in the same way that the large cats are able to, except that they require years of experience to become coordinated, while humans will be able to summarize everything they've learned in just a few phrases. And as their linguistic skills improve, the organization of these groups will become more complex. But not until fireside storytelling becomes a feature will human communities really start to grow bigger. The stories and legends they share extend the bonds between the members of a tribe, enabling one single explanation for the world, and thereby a shared vision. It will provide them with a past that is theirs alone, certain legendary events that paint them as heroes and make them stronger as a people, shared aspirations and a collective mission – the same for everyone. Thus, the first societies begin to take form. Mythical thinking will give rise to religions, which in turn will give us an identity to set us apart from other peoples, as well as gods for whom to fight without fear of death. It is the only way to function as an army of ants while at the same time conserving an amount of individual liberty. The sense of belonging will engender all manner of patriotic symbols, emblems and flags. Various truths will be invented which simultaneously unite and separate, mythical beliefs upon which national identities can be founded. Myths to do with race, gender, social norms, customs, rights and laws, inheritance, history, science – myths that will always be dressed up as the truth while having little or nothing to do with it. You can get cohesiveness on the basis of just about anything, from membership of a social class, a club, a neighbourhood, a company, right up to supporting a certain sports team, even with the changing over time of players, presidents, sponsors and even the crest or team strip. This mythical thinking – so coarse, so primitive – is at the same time the thing that has driven us to impose ourselves on all the other species of the planet: to try to be better than all the other animals, to the point of dominating, subjugating and plundering them, even to the point of extinction.

And we still haven't considered the third factor that comes in with the use of lies, and without which the emergence of civilizations would not have been possible. Civic-mindedness itself is entirely the result of our capacity for deception.

How could we have tolerated living alongside the other, had we known what they really thought about us? Who could possibly tolerate life in society if they had to reveal continuously what was really going through their mind? Would any gathering of people at all be possible if none of them could rein in their emotions, if we weren't possessed of the faculty of being able to feel one thing and say something else altogether?

Good manners, decorum, the norms of courtesy and neighbourliness are all rooted in our willingness to modulate the ongoing deception. Having dealings with other people means staying in a constant state of dissimulation

– the one that means us trying to put our best foot forward. So that other people will stand me, I have to smile and be agreeable, even though I'm not feeling precisely happy inside.

'How are you?' The question can come from any stranger in a lift or someone serving us in a shop, in accordance with the basic formulae of politeness.

'I'm good', we will lie.

And nobody in the world will even consider a response like:

> 'I'm feeling really sad, actually. I've been feeling down, utterly depressed, for years. Ever since I found out that my work isn't fulfilling and that I don't have a real vocation. My life lacks meaning, I'm just drifting along. I also didn't sleep a wink last night, because I ate something that disagreed with me yesterday and spent the whole night running back and forth to the toilet with horrible diarrhoea. How about you? I'm after a white shirt. For a wedding. I'm going on my own.'

From the very first settlements to megalopolises, all human progress is maintained by association and, therefore, by social lying. We need it and depend on it every minute of every day. When I smile, when I nod, when I say, 'No, no, I don't mind picking the kids up between my meeting at five o'clock and the next one at six.' We lie when we put make-up on; when we consider what clothes we're going to wear today; when we walk confidently between the tables on a packed bar terrace; when we sit up straight and, though exhausted, stop ourselves from collapsing on the armchair. Back nice and straight. We lie when we gesticulate, when we admit that somebody is right, when we speak euphemistically, when we follow the crowd or pretend we find something funnier than we actually do. In general, we try to keep other people happy and we like it when other people do the same for us. And if someone acts disagreeably, it makes us want to reject them and we say they are behaving like an imbecile, because that is certainly what they are. Lying is a show of intelligence, the clearest sign of intelligence. And without a sense of empathy, civilization would never have got off the ground. Some people shield themselves with absolute sincerity and by voicing everything they think, claiming that this makes them more authentic, while in reality it shows nothing but clumsiness, a lack of competence in understanding a complex reality, a clear symptom of regression.

'Don't you like it?' asks the dinner host looking down at the plate of food you've left virtually untouched.

'No, it's completely disgusting. I've never liked pumpkin, or this green stuff over here. And meat cooked like this makes me want to puke. By the way, your house is pretty disgusting too, did you decorate it yourself?'

It is likely that such non-lying conduct – in the days when people still sat down to eat together with swords or guns at their sides, and when there still weren't laws in place to keep us safe – would have led humanity to a far more uncertain future. Or to outright extinction, as in fact happened with other advanced hominids. From the moment intelligence emerged as an evolutionary trait, it became quite pressing to introduce new conditions and provisions for the protection of some thinking subjects from others through the masks of simulation. *Sapiens sapiens*.

And it isn't only a question of courtesy – far from it. Lying also becomes essential when we are faced with danger. It isn't only beneficial in creating friendship ties – when, for example, your friend neglects to admit that he's with you out of pure self-interest – it would also be impossible to stand shoulder to shoulder with somebody who has confessed they would flee the field of battle at the first opportunity, use you as a shield if they saw an arrow heading their way, and who would never, not under any circumstances, carry you out of harm's way if you got wounded. Armies would fall apart in an instant. Which might be a good thing, if there weren't any other armies around made up of troops with a better capacity for lying.

Cohesion by way of deceit is present at all levels of society. Lying is essential for us to coexist with strangers; to have faith in those who hunt, fight or work alongside you; to keep friendships going; and even to form the most basic and intimate bonds inside the family unit.

'For years now, I've been thinking about other men every time we go to bed. If I only thought about you, this barren, neglected body of mine would feel nothing.'

'Don't worry, dear. I'm only with you out of habit because I've never found anything better. But that could change at any second.'

Were the social fabric as dysfunctional as this, raising children would be a struggle. As would engendering them, unless by using force.

There is still, however, a greater intimacy than that which is established between couples or with one's parents, and in which mendaciousness also becomes inevitable: the kind that takes place inside our heads.

It would be completely impossible to coexist with other people if we weren't able to deceive ourselves. If every individual did not have the capacity to lie to themselves ahead of anybody else, they would never put up with the proximity of others. In order to tolerate being pitched together with other people, we must make use of at least two forms of lying: the hiding of secrets and self-deception.

In the first place – hiding what we are thinking, not telling people what we've got in mind or saying the complete opposite to what we are thinking – these can be the only way of maintaining the most elemental privacy, the one that goes on this side of our skull. If we were forced to confess all our secrets, if we couldn't keep a lid on things, or pretend, or lie about what's going on inside us, we'd never get as far as living alongside others, and just end up wandering the desert like coyotes. Life in society is possible, first and foremost, because we are able to keep this sphere of intimacy untouched by other people. And human relations, almost in their entirety, are based on what we do and do not know about others. In war, business, politics, love. Even when we claim to open up, we still lie to some degree. And this lie is nothing less than the indispensable precondition for freedom. Our actions sometimes give us away, but the only way to extract the things we keep inside our heads is by threat or coercion, by using torture, or through lie detectors or a truth serum.

Because who could possibly accept us as we really are? Not even ourselves. Least of all ourselves.

And because of that, second, we are obliged to employ the psychological strategy of self-deceit. In a world – whether natural or artificial – that rewards lying, the logical thing would be to come to the conclusion that believing in our own fictions gives us an advantage, since it helps us pass them off to other people with greater conviction. And though, in large measure, this is true, the impulses that drive us to deceive ourselves are more complicated still. Our minds work not only with concepts, but with emotions as well. And emotions are something particularly difficult to manage, from the moment we wake up in the morning and throughout the time we remain conscious. It isn't so much that we dislike our reality, as a rejection on the part of our innermost selves, which are the filter through which we view our reality and something we can never escape. Wherever we go, the self is there. In the shape of our memories, things we've done in the past, our present failings, our stubborn problems. The need we feel to escape from ourselves is the reason why people in every single society have tried to get high in one way or another; and, in those rare places where they have found no substance that will do the job, they've tried restricting their oxygen intake, taking running leaps down steep hills, and dancing for days on end until they attain the escape they so yearn for. We can't stand ourselves. We find our own presence insufferable, even though we come fitted with a mechanism to help to cover up imperfections. And even though, thanks to self-deception, we are able to form an unrealistically favourable picture of ourselves. We overestimate ourselves, we dress up the facts, we are very good at selective hearing, we tell ourselves half-truths, we skip the bits of our own stories that don't interest us; we also have a selective memory in the sense that we forget painful memories and generally massage the facts; we cook up fantasies for every aspect of our life; we continuously repeat bits of information that benefit us, making them a little bit better every time, and, in general, elaborate a mental image of ourselves in a more flattering light than how we appear in the mirror and in photographs. And still we can't stand ourselves. Sometimes, depending on the day, depending on the personality, we also deceive ourselves in the other direction, by underestimating ourselves. But the opposite is far more usual. Between 80 per cent and 95 per cent of all qualified professionals think they do a better job than any of their colleagues. And when we ask anyone if they think they've had a fair crack at life, whether professionally or in whatever their specialism happens to be, those percentages go even higher. We all think we are better than outward recognition would suggest. We all think that, compared to other people, we've been on the receiving end of some kind of bad luck, some injustice or grievance. And among those who enjoy the plaudits that come with success and recognition, none will say they think less of themselves than others do; nobody calls their own achievements a fraud or the result of sheer chance. And yet this is quite natural. We wouldn't even be able to address ourselves with total sincerity. Nobody in a healthy state of mind and whose spirits aren't low, however alone they might be in a room, would ever stand in front of the mirror and say:

> My blood is still boiling from that argument a few moments ago, but I know I'm in the wrong. I am a pig. I've twisted the arguments out of pure egotism, because I'm an egoist utterly incapable of shouldering the blame for anything. I always blame other people. And yes, if I've hurt people along the way, it's because it makes me feel better; someone else feeling bad gives me a sense of relief, of wellbeing. My personality is pretty repugnant, pretty despicable.

There is a limit to our capacity for self-criticism. And as much as one might wish to submit to it, there would be many things one would never say because they are actually beyond what we can imagine. Some processes of self-deceit are more or less conscious; defects we discovered years ago but mostly managed to overlook, to block out; feelings of guilt that we do our best not to stir up; parts of ourselves we've managed to confess in moments of weakness, but that we deny when we're feeling okay again; decisions we always put off for the next day. There are many others, however, that slip beneath the threshold of our awareness. Ones we have no control over and the nature of which we couldn't even guess at. They stay hidden in the deepest reaches of the unconscious. Luckily for us.

The brain itself is designed to maintain the equilibrium. Lying is something so necessary and – in certain cases – so healthy, since it regulates our organism in moments of crisis. A depressed mind means we drop our defences, it pushes us into morbid thinking, weakens the immune system, exposes us to illness and shortens our lifespan. Strong, healthy bodies depend on a happy, self-deceived mind.

So now we can finally establish an idea that more resembles our true situation.

Humans are caught up in a mesh of lies. In a universe that turns on lies, in a society built on lies, and in a biology created by lies.

Hence why all human activity is linked to the act of lying.

WAR AND STRATEGY

In the sixth century before Christ, the Chinese strategist Sun Tzu declared in *The Art of War* that all warfare is based on deception. When you are on the offensive, he said, make it seem like you've got a handicap. If your army is ready and your troops are on the move, seem inactive. When you are planning an attack in the vicinity of the enemy line, make as though you are preparing for a long march. When your plan is to attack a distant point, pretend that your target is nearby. Discourage your enemy by making your own victory seem likely; surprise him by creating confusion. Set traps, offer bait to entice your enemy. If he is secure at all points, be prepared to fight; if he is superior in strength, evade him. A military force uses deception when it deploys, mobilizes by promising illusory rewards, and triumphs by use of division and confusion.

In the war against the Huns, an emperor in the Han Dynasty sent ten scouts to go and spy on the invaders. And all of them alike came back and said that an attack on the Huns was entirely feasible. The emperor then sent one final spy by the name of Lou Jing. When he came back, unlike those who had gone previously, this scout declared that no attack on the Hun hordes could possibly have a positive outcome.

'What makes you think that?' the emperor wanted to know.

'When two forces are equally matched, they will seek to make themselves seem stronger than they are', he said. 'But all the soldiers I saw on my mission were weak and old. This shows that they are making a show of incompetence. And because of that, I would not recommend an attack.'

It goes without saying that, when the emperor heard this, he flew into a rage and had Lou Jing thrown in prison for obstructing the interests of the empire with such foolishness. He then called up the greatest contingent he had at his disposal and placed himself at its head, bent on finishing off the nomadic invaders once and for all. When they made to advance, however, they found themselves surrounded by thousands upon thousands of Huns, who hemmed them in and cut off their supply lines, until eventually the emperor had to admit defeat.

During the Second World War, in 1943, at a military base in Tennessee, the 23rd Headquarters Special Troops began a recruitment drive. It would go on to comprise three units specializing in deception: the 603rd Camouflage Engineers, which was tasked with visual strategies; the Special Effect Company, responsible for sonic deception; and the Signal Company, which created phony traffic nets – or 'Spoof radio', as it was called – impersonating the radio operators from real units. In a matter of months, this tactical unit consisted of more than 1,000 engineers, architects, designers, actors and artists from art schools in New York and Philadelphia. PR men were even recruited, with the idea that they would have the talent and imagination to find ways of tricking the enemy.

The epicentre of its first mission was going to be D-Day – namely, convincing the Nazis that the landings would take place not in Normandy but farther to the east. They came up with an array of subterfuges that would make it seem like two entirely fictional regiments of 30,000 soldiers in fact existed. After a number of early abortive prototypes, they succeeded in designing units of *inflatable* tanks, trucks, jeeps and artillery; these could be transported effortlessly and blown up in just a few minutes, and their passing would leave no trace. The camps would be made up of tents without any soldiers inside, the wooden ammo boxes would be empty, the canisters contain not a drop of petrol. Recordings had also been made at Fort Knox, with the help of the engineers from Bell Laboratories, so that the sound of different military vehicles, artillery shots and soldiers building portable bridges could be played. And, last of all, actors were dressed up as members of the top brass, and their job would be to confirm the imminent arrival of the main body of the army.

And so, along with the real Sherman tanks, Dodge trucks and actual artillery, other suitcase-sized packages began arriving in England. The contents of these, once blown up with pumps, would become highly convincing imitations; the turrets on the tanks even had pretend rivets. The ghost army was positioned at various strategic places on the map in order to make the German forces spread along the whole length of the coast, thereby weakening the defence at the point in Normandy where the attack was planned. The idea was to make Hitler believe that the largest disembarkation would happen farther along the coast, around Calais. The Signal Company started transmitting an array of related radio messages, some in code and some not, from false orders to confirmations of the arrival of various detachments. Every angle had been covered: a number of priests in East Anglia wrote to local newspapers complaining about the terrible behaviour of locally stationed, non-existent foreign troops. The inflatable tanks and other vehicles were left poorly camouflaged, so that they could be spotted from the air. The sound recordings played through gigantic amplifiers could be heard at a distance of 24 km. Finally, General Patton was asked to go to England and let himself be photographed, to reinforce the rumour that he would be at the head of this grand, entirely bogus army.

The operation was a success. The Germans indeed sent out messages saying they were expecting the arrival of a large Allied fleet in Calais and Dunkirk. The subterfuge never came to light. The 23rd Headquarters Special Troops carried on their work throughout the rest of the war, notching up a total of twenty ghost missions. In a large number of them, the sham soldiers actually attracted more enemy fire than they would have wanted.

In war, secrets and lies are so valuable that the story of this tactical unit was only revealed more than fifty years after the fact. And many of its details remain classified to this day.

ESPIONAGE AND COUNTER-ESPIONAGE

Every head of state, statesperson, military person and strategist knows the importance of lies when it comes to international rivalries, and indeed war. They also therefore know that it is essential to have knowledge of one's enemy's secrets, in order to be able to anticipate their lies with your own. From the moment the leader of any group sends a scout to spy on another group, they show us that human battles begin, first of all, at a hypothetical level. But our capacity for schemes and intrigues is such that the lies can immediately begin to pile up, and everything become so tangled that we lose the thread. At this point, espionage becomes counter-espionage. All intelligence services, from the FBI and the CIA to the now-defunct KGB, from Mossad to the Spanish CNI, all have their own counter-espionage and counter-intelligence units, whose aim is to avoid the enemy obtaining secret or compromising information and, in general, to create a smokescreen of disinformation. And then cryptography, concealment through codes, undercover operations, deception techniques, double agents and countersurveillance come into play: rather than arrest those suspected of spying, it is far more advantageous to watch them in order to establish what they know, what they are plotting, where they are going and with whom they are having their assignations.

And the game, to paraphrase Kipling, ceases neither day nor night.

In fact, the success of all the chicanery that threw the Nazis off the scent of the D-Day landings wasn't down to the 23rd Headquarters Special Troops alone. A Spanish agent named Joan Pujol was also crucial in this. Known to the Germans by the code name 'Alaric' and to the British as 'Garbo', his story and his capacity for artifice – far-fetched though it may seem – might just be even more surprising.

Born in Barcelona in 1914, during the Spanish Civil War his Catholic family was treated harshly by the Republicans, who arrested his mother and his sister on charges of counter-revolutionary activities. As a young man, Pujol managed to desert and join the Nationalists, but he was later arrested and beaten by his colonel for being pro-monarchy. Both facts would go on to play a significant role in his future: the contempt he felt for fascism and communism alike became an animus against Nazi Germany and the USSR, and he decided to fight both in exactly the way he had fought to date – that is, without firing a single bullet. In 1940, in the early days of the Second World War, with Franco bedding in, he took the first steps towards joining Great Britain in its opposition to the Third Reich. He approached the British on as many as three separate occasions, but they showed no interest in recruiting him as a spy. So he went and offered his services to Germany, passing himself off as a civil servant in the Spanish government, and fanatically pro-Nazi at that – all the while intending to work for the Allies as a double agent. He was soon taken on by German intelligence. They gave him a fast-track course in espionage, taught him how to write in code and sent him off on his first mission: he was to travel to Great Britain and recruit a network of agents in the service of the Reich. Joan

Pujol, however, had no intention of installing himself in the British Isles – firstly, because he didn't speak the language; and secondly, because nothing about his plan required him to be there. Instead, he went and set up in Lisbon and, never leaving the city – availing himself of a UK travel book, magazines from a public library and any news items he caught at the cinema – began to travel the length and breadth of Britain in his imagination. On the basis of this, he began sending made-up reports to the Germans on the movements of boats, followed by equally made-up travel expenses. He began weaving a network of completely fictitious sub-agents. His reports were intercepted and the fact they completely contradicted anything that was actually going on drew the attention of British counter-intelligence, who then set out on a no-expenses-spared plan to recruit Pujol. Despite this, he soon contacted them himself. And at this point, in April 1942, he was officially taken on as a double agent for the Allies.

To begin with, he continued in the direction of travel he had established in Lisbon. His main focus was maintaining the charade of his network of agents. Some of these agents were supposedly influential individuals in possession of highly valuable information. Among his fictional spies were William Gerbers, a Swiss-German impresario; Dagobert, a Welsh nationalist heading up the fascist Brothers of the Aryan World Order in Swansea; Chamillus, a Gibraltarian waiter living in Chislehurst, London; Benedict, a Venezuelan student in Glasgow; Benedict's sister, Moonbeam, who lived in Ottawa, Canada; and a cousin of Moonbeam and Benedict who lived in Buffalo, New York . . . As one might expect, the difficulty lay in having to come up with a constant stream of reports from each of these characters, and making them add up. By the end, he had invented twenty-seven different agents. There were times when he had to explain why one of his spies had failed to alert them to operations after the fact. He might claim they had fallen ill just before a significant naval manoeuvre, and had on occasion to kill them off, leaving more than one imaginary widow to collect the pension for a fallen agent. The widows, naturally, were automatically incorporated into Garbo's group.

Who could have guessed that the Spanish spy named Joan Pujol would go on to be among the twenty people in the world who knew in advance the date and the exact location of the D-Day landings?

In January 1944, the Germans had communicated to him that they were anticipating a large-scale invasion in Europe and asked him to pass them any relevant information. This was how Pujol became part of the machinations aimed at confounding Hitler: his job now was to make him believe that the Allied invasion would take place in Calais, and that manoeuvres around Normandy would be no more than subterfuge intended to divert the German forces. Pujol put his tangled web of non-existent spies to work. And from that time until D-Day, he would send over 500 radio messages, sometimes more than 20 a day and at all hours, giving information on the constant arrival of American and Canadian troops in British ports. The Führer fell for the whole thing, sending sixteen German divisions to the Scandinavian coast, where they would sit doing absolutely nothing until mid-June. Come 6 June, however, the Spaniard, with Eisenhower's blessing, had no option but to inform the Nazis of the Allied landing in Normandy – to avoid his cover being blown. He did so at 4 a.m. in a coded message. It took the Germans at least another four hours to receive the message, decode it and pass it up the ranks recoded. By then, the invasion was already under way.

Hitler himself would go on to send a message of congratulations to Alaric, thanking him for the information and services provided. And, to the day he died, the German chancellor would continue to believe that the Allies landed in Normandy rather than Calais only because of a last-minute change of plan.

On 29 July 1944, Alaric was awarded the Iron Cross for extraordinary services to the Fatherland.

On 25 November 1944, Garbo received an MBE from King George VI.

Joan Pujol was the first person to receive both distinctions.

Five years later, after separating from his wife, with whom he'd had three children, he was certified as having died from malaria in Angola. Nonetheless, although no thinking subject outside his skull would know it – not even the British intelligence services – his death was yet another of his impostures. With the money he earned in the war – he managed to get the Nazi government to pay his imaginary agents a total of US$340,000 – after feigning his own death, he moved to Venezuela, where he opened a bookshop, remarried and had another three children. His Spanish family had no idea he was still alive. His Venezuelan family had no idea who he had been. In light moments, he confessed to them that he was a former secret agent.

'I was the spy who toppled the Third Reich', he would say.

'Where? In Europe?'

'Of course, I was the man who saved the world.' (This was what the international press would go on to dub him in later years.)

'How did you do that, then?'

'With my imagination.'

And they would all laugh.

Only one person would think to doubt such a novelistic ending in Angola, the kind belonging to someone bent on disappearing. It was the spy novel-writer Nigel West – novelists understand better than anyone the fictional nature of reality – who in the 1970s embarked on an investigation that would take more than a decade to come to completion. He interviewed various former agents from military intelligence, to no avail; nobody seemed to know Garbo's real name. Finally, in the spring of 1984, he tracked him down. And, not long after, managed to arrange a meeting in New Orleans with the double agent who had risen from the dead as a real person.

After that conversation, Joan Pujol decided to make a trip to London, where he was given a hero's welcome at Buckingham Palace.

His children – both sets – found out who he really was in the newspapers.

POLITICAL LIES

Politics, as a man once put it, is the art of convincing the people of salutary falsehoods for some good end.

This same man, a few paragraphs earlier, had begun his reflection by speaking about how human beings are physiologically predisposed to lying, before going on to say that an art as useful and noble as lying ought to have, like the rest of the disciplines, its own dedicated entry in encyclopaedias, which would then serve as a guide to all politicians who hoped for future glory. With a subtle sense of irony, he carried on into a possible classification of the lies most used by the politicians of his time, and numerous pieces of advice to help people's lies work better, spread more quickly and last longer. When he finished, he gave a semi-satisfied smile, briefly drummed his fingers on the desk and titled his short treatise *The Art of Political Lying* (1712).

However, as though lying itself had been angered by this individual for revealing the ploys used by its most noteworthy ambassadors on earth – political men and demagogues – and had cursed him for it, somewhere on the journey from his desk to the printers his name went astray and never made it on to the cover of the book. Over the three ensuing centuries, this essay would be falsely attributed to Jonathan Swift. Not such an unexpected slip as it might seem, because Swift was a long-standing friend of the true author; both were also writers whose work was steeped in irony. Admittedly, one was Irish and one Scottish. And the latter was called John Arbuthnot and didn't, it seems, exist inside Swift's body, but rather – like everyone – trapped inside his own head.

Politics is the art of convincing the people of salutary falsehoods for some good end, Arbuthnot once said.[1]

And it is true that the debate about whether or not the truth ought to be kept from citizens for their own sake – whether, in order to protect them, you need to mislead them – has always been around, since the emergence of politics itself. It was a question posed long before the Enlightenment, something thinkers have batted around from the times of the Greek *polis*, from the days of Plato's *Republic* and Aristotle's *Politics*. And, given the conduct of governments around the world today, we can hardly say that it has gone away.

But we do need to zoom out a long way to tackle the problem properly. If, as we have seen, lying is part and parcel of everything humans do, it will therefore be a part of politics in a far more profound sense. And not only because

[1] It would take another 300 years for John Arbuthnot's authorship to come to light. Yet everything seems to point to the impossibility of thumbing one's nose against lying, or making incursions into the lands of untruth, and coming away unscathed. A Spanish publishing house recently put out a new, bilingual edition of *The Art of Political Lying*. It was all very carefully and thoughtfully done, with a prologue that finally cleared up the misunderstanding for Spanish readers and gave back to poor, mistreated Arbuthnot his rightful paternity of the essay. Nonetheless, quite incredibly – perhaps because of the unpronounceable surname, questions of marketing trickery or other reasons that in any case the publishing house does not explain – the cover of the book once more figures but a single name, and in nice, big lettering: Jonathan Swift.

it has always been considered a necessary and justifiable tool for the work of men of state in their role as guardians for the great ingenuous unwashed. Take a moment to consider the earliest and most optimistic evaluations, and we immediately see that deception was already intrinsic in classical definitions: politics is an activity that uses words and persuasion to convince others of something that affects us all. Precisely: an attempt to mislead others via the use of metaphor to make them create their own fictions. And next, when history led us to doubt the human condition, not only did the most pessimistic and Machiavellian types not give up on such attempts at persuasion, they sought to do so by force: the prince must impose himself by the use of power, because politics consists in intervening in conflicts between people, and opposed interests and visions of the world.

Lying, therefore, is found equally in the two possible versions of politics: the one that is based on cooperation; and the other, on conflict. The only difference being whether the will of the powerful is brought to bear through rhetoric or coercion.

Both of these political tendencies – the one that seeks consensus, and the one that bases itself on our antagonisms – have coexisted ever since we became social beings. Even in primates with no linguistic capacities, it's possible to see individuals winning the group over purely through leadership, while others use violence and brute strength to dominate. Mythical and religious thinking came down on the side of charismatic domination; in patriarchies and feudal situations, strength is what matters; while nation states learned to create a monopoly on legitimate violence within a certain territory. And these three kinds of relationship between ruler and ruled have been in operation, in different measure, throughout history, up to and including the present day – if we take into account the crisis faced by the church at the end of the Middle Ages, culminating in the Great East–West Schism of 1378 and prompting root-and-stem structural reorganization in the powerhouses of the time – France, Spain, England – which in turn led those nations to become the modern European states we now know.[2] With the decline of Christianity's powers of persuasion, the institutions underlying these monarchies reorganized around another old acquaintance: war. In the Renaissance, the principal requirement of any European monarch was to have an army, to the point where royal revenue was almost entirely consumed by military demands. Thus, the military machine created a structure of fiscal support around itself, taking in consultants, tax collectors, inspectors – all of which would give rise to what we know as modern-day bureaucracy. The church, quickly seeing the new situation for what it was – something that relegated it to the background – in order to conserve a modicum of power and control over the sovereignty of monarchs, hurried to give its blessing to these new entities, legitimating their authority by divine right. This accreditation, which the respective monarchs exploited in their own ways, also gave rise to a new literary subgenre known as mirrors for princes: tracts and treatises that set out to extol the virtues of rulers – their wisdom, justice, magnanimity and prudence.

The Florentine thinker Niccolò Machiavelli had a clear-eyed view of the situation, and never considered the

[2] Far earlier precedents of nation states nonetheless exist – when the term is understood as institutional organizations that capture the legal power to coerce people: Ancient Egypt, the Roman Empire, Imperial China, Byzantium and the Ottoman Empire would be some examples.

church an enemy of the state. On the contrary, he knew that, if skilfully deployed, it could be used by those in power to guarantee the obedience of their subjects. And yet Machiavelli always viewed politics from an antagonistic perspective. In the 'mirror' he wrote in 1531, *The Prince*, he made quite clear his view that anyone wishing to get into politics must go down the path of evil and be prepared to renounce ethics for the sake of greater goals. He contended that man is wicked by nature, moved by egotism, self-interest and his own wellbeing alone, and that his ambitions compel him to all kinds of criminal acts. And it therefore follows that the starting point for any head of state is to assume that, in all its dealings with others, they will demonstrate this duplicitousness at the first opportunity, and so to be prepared for all eventualities. The prince should have no compunction about dishonourable acts of cruelty, as the very saving of his kingdom may depend on them. Questions of what is just or unjust simply shouldn't come into it for the prince, who has only to choose the way ahead that will save his kingdom. The ends, in other words, always justify the means. The prince can act against faith, charity, humanity, religion, but he must never say anything that in the eyes of others could fail to make him appear good, upstanding, humane and religious.

What is crucial, ultimately, isn't that the prince possesses these qualities – which, in fact, would be to his disadvantage. Rather, it is that he appears to possess them. Everyone will see what you seem to be, declared Machiavelli, but few will understand what you really are.

And, of course, he provided a better elucidation than any of the need for imposture, and the lying aspect crucial to all politics:

> For some time I have never said what I believed and never believed what I said, and if I do sometimes happen to say what I think, I always hide it among so many lies that it is hard to recover. (Letter to Governor Francesco Guicciardini, 1521)

None of this is to suggest that nation states always arise out of totalitarianism purely because they have a monopoly on the invention of norms and the public use of force. There are many possible models for the state, and lies and violence are part of all of them, though in different proportions.

In the freest societies, among the many means for the supervision of the populace, governments of course prioritize techniques of deception and manipulation.

Meanwhile, at the despotic end of the spectrum, governments don't bother to explain their lies, but choose rather to impose them by force.

In *The Art of Political Lying*, John Arbuthnot tried to analyse the different kinds of deception used by the politicians of his day – eighteenth-century parliamentarian England – where the parties that currently vie for power there were already facing off. He came up with three types of fallacy in this arena: the 'detractory, or defamatory', which 'takes from a great man the reputation that justly belongs to him, for fear he should use it to the detriment of the publick'; the 'additory', which 'gives to a great man a larger share of reputation than belongs to him, to enable him to serve some good end or purpose'; and the 'translatory', which 'transfers the merit of a man's good action to another, who is in himself more deserving; or transfers the demerit of a bad action from the true author to a person, who is in himself less deserving'. When lies are directed towards the public rather than politicians, he pinpoints other kinds: 'terrifying lies', which 'should not be too frequently shown to the people, lest they grow familiar'; 'animating or encouraging lies', which 'should not far exceed the common degrees of probability; that there should be variety of them; and the same lie not obstinately insisted upon'; and 'promissory lies', which one can tell because they come with 'shouldering, hugging, squeezing, smiling, bowing'.

Arbuthnot also pondered the means politicians had at their disposal in order to invent, spread and multiply the lies they could tell. In his day, however, these never went beyond broadsides and slanderous jokes. It wouldn't be long before the Industrial Revolution came along and made the pasquinades pinned up in the squares seem positively mediaeval. The invention of Linotype and the development of the written press meant moving beyond speech as the main source of defamation, and lies spreading with previously unseen speed and effectiveness. Of course, governments, who are the only ones with the legal right to coin official lies, always made sure to keep a grip on the newspapers. In the twentieth century, with the arrival of mass media, and specifically television, the reach became so wide that it would have been unimaginable before. And this would go further still when smartphones became commonplace in the first decade of our century, and this new technology delivered such untruths directly to every pocket and handbag, every bedside table, and to the palms of every citizen's hand.

Compared with the lies of the twenty-first century, Arbuthnot's typology will strike us as naïve and overly trusting. But how could he have imagined that the publicity techniques of the post-industrial era would be put at the service of political propaganda? Though it might seem fairly normal to us, there was a time when political candidates didn't have their own marketing teams dedicated solely to studying the spectrum of the electorate; to writing their speeches; to working out how, by tweaking an electoral programme, more votes can be won; to designing strategies and buying up slots in the media; to analysing the chinks in the opposition's armour; and to schooling their candidate on how to speak and gesticulate, what to read, how not to stumble when there are cameras around, what not to say, what to wear and how to wear make-up. Such excessive artifice and vain simulation would have been enough to unsettle even someone stopping by from the time of the Enlightenment. Who from that era could have foreseen digital technologies and their capacity to transform reality? The average person nowadays can't even trust what she sees with her own eyes. And on the net to end all nets – with its inexhaustible, constantly forking paths – all truths and all their opposites live side by side without anybody so much as batting an eyelid.

In the free world, when it comes to imposing their version of the truth, governments have more instruments at their disposal than ever before, which makes the use of force unnecessary. They have an almost limitless variety of means of manipulation, even if these all have to pass through the first premise: people accepting that this manipulation is something both natural and inevitable. The complexity of advanced societies has itself become another thing to be harnessed in governmental misinformation, because the sheer amount of data, so much hyperreality, is confusing for individuals, and facilitates a dense and tangled mesh in which to hide the fraud. In the tortuous tangle of our new reality, it is nigh on impossible to keep track of a lie that has been properly dressed up.

And, what is more, if governments get caught lying, nothing happens anyway.[3]

Minimal democracies have developed coercive structures which make it impossible for the average citizen to play a part in even the most insignificant political decisions. These are mostly 'particracies' – perversions of democracy that reduce the freedom of the electorate, so they always have to 'vote' for the same self-serving oligarchy. This oligarchy de facto hoards all the power, making an appearance of democratic process through periodic but orchestrated exchanges of power between the main political parties – that is, the citizen can only choose between A and B, though neither option is worthy or satisfactory. If this reduction of people's political capacity weren't enough, should the elected government then fail to deliver the entirety of its electoral programme – which is all the citizens can vote for every four years – still nothing will happen. The vertical

[3] In 2002, the United States and United Kingdom initiated a propaganda campaign – Spain would later join in – claiming that there were weapons of mass destruction (WMD) in Iraq. Though reports from the Senate Select Committee on Intelligence judged that 'Iraq unilaterally destroyed its undeclared chemical weapons stockpile in 1991. . .. [And] [t]here are no credible indications that Baghdad resumed production of chemical munitions thereafter', the people running these countries went ahead with the campaign. And with WMD as their excuse, they proceeded to invade Iraq in March 2003, and Saddam Hussein was toppled. These democratic governments needed the threat of WMD as justification, because imposing a regime change in another country would have been legally impermissible. More than eight years of war followed on from the invasion. The WMD never emerged. According to a report by the Center for Public Integrity, between 2001 and 2003 the Bush government notched up a total of 935 false statements to do with the supposed threat posed by Iraq to the United States. The war resulted in a humanitarian crisis with human rights abuses and more than 1 million people dead, mostly Iraqi civilians. And, despite all this, at the time of writing, these lies still haven't brought any penal or political consequences for the leaders of the governments involved.

control mechanisms have been deactivated. Because the political class holds all the cards in the creating of laws, these will never be directed at the oligarch, but only at the citizen who criticizes the system. Laws are never made, for example, that would condemn political leaders for associating with economic powers for their own good and to the detriment of public interest; in contrast, all of the state's coercive power will be brought to bear on citizens who use civil disobedience to point out systemic corruption. In these models, of course, the system is the truth.

Yes, politics is the art of convincing the people of salutary falsehoods, for some good end. But whose good? Nobody said it had to be that of the public. In minimal democracies, the 'good end' of lies is nothing but the personal gain of politicians.

The difference between these weak democracies with minimal participation and the third political possibility, that of totalitarian models, is that the latter exercise violence in a far more bloody and generalized fashion. And, unlike the previous examples, on this side of the scales there is barely any need to hide who really decides what is true and what is false.

We should not, however, forget that there is still one more fundamental aspect that defines all totalitarian systems: and it is that, under them, nobody is free to choose their own lies.

The totalitarian system imposes one single lie. It does this through complete control of the press and all media channels, leaving its fingerprints on all the stories constructed in relation to present-day reality and events. To this same end, literature, art and all symbol-making are closely supervised, like the great generators of fiction that they are. And special attention will be paid to rewriting history in specific ways. Lastly, the most extreme aspiration for totalitarianism is always to break the individual liberty of every woman and man, knocking down the protective barrier of their inner lies and seeking to have a hand in their fantasies, dreams and personal fictions.

Nobody should be able to impose falsehoods on us. We all have a right to choose which lies we believe.

BUSINESS AND ECONOMICS

With his 1987 film *Wall Street*, Oliver Stone perhaps did more than anyone to make Sun Tzu's *Art of War* fashionable among economists. In the 1990s, a wide array of stockbrokers, investors, businessmen, young entrepreneurs and highly motivated wannabe exchange traders – whose forays into literature tended not to go beyond stock indexes and profitability studies – would unexpectedly adopt this 2,500-year-old manual on military tactics as their bedtime reading. And they have gone on doing so into the present day, which gives us an idea of the theoretical and humanist underpinnings of the financial world. And, above all, of the general focus of economics over the last century.

Nonetheless, long before economics and military strategy became so intimately linked, lying sat at the heart of the most elemental business practices.

Barter and exchange first arose, in fact, between rival communities; we have no documented cases of such interchange within members of a single clan. When the early settlements of farmer-agriculturalists first began to find themselves with free time on their hands, the human imagination could not help but get drawn into the fashioning of new products, inventing tools and contraptions, making ceramics, knick-knacks and *objets d'art*. So, our imaginative excesses bubbled over in the form of material surplus – the creation of things that may not be consumed as such, and that will later go on to be called wealth. At that time, these goods would have been equally shared out within a community, and there was no such thing as private property yet, and so these surpluses would have been used to acquire things that were more needed from a rival clan. Hence, barter and exchange came about in a context of mistrust and competitiveness, with opposing sides trying to obtain the greatest possible advantage over one another, to avoid being had, and to negotiate with their respective self-interests foremost.

We read in Herodotus of the Carthaginians unloading goods on the Libyan coast, having sailed through the Pillars of Hercules (most likely this is the Gold Coast of what is now known as Ghana, if we take Libya to be Africa and the Pillars of Hercules the Gibraltar Strait), and leaving them spread out there on the sandy beach. They then went back to their boats and announced their presence with a column of smoke. The indigenous peoples would go down to the shore, examine the goods and leave alongside them as much gold as they thought fair payment. Then the indigenous people would go away, the Carthaginians land once more and take a look at the offer. If they considered it acceptable, they would gather up the gold and sail on; if not, they would leave it there – along with the goods – and go back to the boats to await a better offer. This kind of 'silent commerce', or 'mute bartering', made haggling possible between peoples who spoke different languages. And a similar system had very likely been in operation before the capacity for language itself arose – it is the same universal procedure used by the Mbuti people when exchanging meat for bananas with the Bantus, and by the Inuit in Alaska, and the Bulu and Pygmies in southern Cameroon.

The starting context is always one of scepticism, in which any of the parties is susceptible to deceit. And, in fact, the only time any of the respective parties is safe from fraud is when there is the goal of establishing long-term relations. Because, if this isn't the case, the gift initially deposited in the environs of a foreign people, in the hope of some gesture in kind, could just be nothing but bait.

The Phoenicians, who traded throughout the Mediterranean, and did so in entirely reputable ways that led to the establishment of long-lasting ties, were at the same time slavers. And there is every chance that the slaves, before becoming slaves, were nothing but overly trusting foreigners – the more credulous kind who probably hung around the bait, rather than withdrawing somewhere safe. Whereas, in places where people were more cautious about their safety, and where the Phoenicians were interested in settling and maintaining relations with the indigenous people, they would set up markets. In all markets that came before the arrival of coinage – those in Egypt, China, Phoenicia, Africa – deceit and haggling were commonplace. The person selling is in it for maximum profit, and it necessarily follows that they claim their products are worth more than they really are. The person buying is then obligated to haggle, this time using hand gestures if they don't speak the same language, and to make a lower offer than they know the product is worth. The person selling will display their merchandise to look as attractive as possible, with the freshest and most eye-catching items at the front, and those in the worst condition hidden at the back. The person buying will exaggerate the imperfections of the article they want, to try and tip the exchange in their favour. The person selling will sing the praises of their goods, extolling their virtues as much as they can, thereby giving rise to the earliest manifestation of proto-publicity.

But later on, when the wealth of the primitive agrarian societies begins to accumulate in the hands of the few, when the division of labour that took shape with the Neolithic (or First Agricultural) Revolution is swept aside by that of the Industrial Revolution – once more increasing the amount of wealth in circulation as well as the distances between people – out of the economic infrastructure a chimerical superstructure emerges: speculative, ideological, political, legal, coercive, and apparently with a life of its own. And, once it has emerged, no single individual will ever be able to tame it.

And it will be a fiction that will go on to hold more weight in the lives of human beings than anything concrete.

The superstructure will give rise, in its early phases, to social classes. And, in its final phases, to the world of finance and speculation – that is, the possibility for the exchange of abstract capital between entirely abstract businesses, multinationals and governments, which act to mask the activities of certain real-life individuals.

The speculative economy will be entirely removed from those men who traded in flint, salt, gold, copper, flaxseed, oil or horses – all things raised, cultivated or extracted by real-life people – while still requiring the abstract value attached to flint, salt, gold, copper, flaxseed, oil or horses. There will be speculation on the value of everything that humans can possibly produce. Everything these humans possess. Even the ground on which these humans live. Because the ground, the water, the air, energy, these all now belong to legal entities, business and nation states. The speculative economy can make it so that the ground on which you live is worth so much that you will need to work your entire life to pay for it. The speculative economy can make it so the value of your work declines to such an extent that you will need to add all the work you do in your lifetime to all the work your partner does in theirs in order to pay for the place you live. The speculative economy can, in the end, make it so that the value of the property you bought with two lifetimes' worth of earnings is so low that your children will inherit new and insurmountable debt.

By means of the immense lie that is the economic, political and legal superstructure of the market, the speculator – who moves like a fish through the water of this fabricated environment – can live a life of luxury and excess without ever having to produce a single thing. All this person need do is lie. Nor does this person have to submit to a work schedule or spend lots of hours in the day lying. A few minutes' lying from time to time will be sufficient for the fictitious price of the flax, oil or horses produced or raised by the sweat of real people's brows either to skyrocket or to plummet. Should it skyrocket, the earnings from the abstract trades that take place on abstract markets will go in the speculator's pocket. Should it plummet, by selling to some intermediary the speculator might also make a profit, but the real producer of the real goods will be ruined. He might not be able to pay the water bill – water now being something that belongs to someone else. He might not be able to pay the taxes levied on the land and roads – which belong to someone else. Perhaps he will lose his house, because that always belonged to some banking entity. Perhaps his children will be taken away. Perhaps he'll end up rotting in jail.

Then this man, in whose destruction governments have been complicit, will ask himself why his field of flax or olive grove, which until the previous day was profitable, is suddenly no good. How is this possible, if he has done nothing but get up early and work from sunrise to sunset, just like his father did, and his father's father before him? What has wrought this change? Has he not been as painstaking as ever in his choice of seeds and fertilizers? Has the weather not been good – was there not a decent crop? And did he not sell to the same buyer he has dealt with since he was a boy?

Really, a different question needs to be asked. Did the real producer of the goods have any say over the lies that were being told about that to which he dedicated his life? He did not. The lies that go to make up the stock market are completely out of his control.

The farmer has the same power over the stock market as a citizen does over political decisions in a sham democracy.

Why, then, do the farmers have to shoulder the legal responsibility for something that rightly lies with others?

Let's not fool ourselves. It isn't only that the great lie of financial speculation has been armour-plated by fantastical entelechies, such as risk premiums, interest rates, subprime credit, floor clauses in variable-rate mortgage agreements, clauses on late-payment interests, public debt, the liquidity crisis, the bailout of the banking system, or inflation.

It is, as we have said, due to the collusion of those who make the laws.

A BRIEF HISTORY OF FORGERY

Human beings are condemned, from their very first act of intellection, to falsify reality in their minds. It follows that the most quintessentially human activities, as we have been seeing, consolidate around lying, and assist in the creation of the cultural superstructure that floats all around us.

Nonetheless, among all the types of deliberate human falsifications, there is at least one that isn't directed towards the realm of the hypothetical, but instead at fabricating concrete material counterfeits.

The expert forger uses imitation so that her works will pass as others, ones that – only inasmuch as they are imitated – we call genuine. And her motivations will be as diverse as all our many fields of activity: from the religious to the economic, the military and the political to, as we will see, the artistic.

The first of these possibilities will arise when mythical thinking produces religion, and when that religion has sufficient adherents. A recently invented religion will quickly need a pool of tangible proof, which will help the sceptics to get on board with the thorny transition from the physical to the metaphysical. This is why the early days of Christianity were spent in the feverish confection of sacred texts that would set it apart from Judaism. That would be followed by the natural selection process involved in the struggle for power: in the second century AD, the Jewish rabbis approved their own canon, admitting to the Tanakh, or Hebrew Bible, only the books before Jesus; whereas in the fourth century AD, the Catholic Church would add to these Old Testament texts the four gospels, adjudging them to offer an unambiguous vision of their beliefs, while rejecting all the other gospels. That is, four were canonized and another fifty-plus were deemed heretical; from this point on, they were known as 'apocryphal'. To begin with, the term 'apocryphal' (from *apo* meaning 'off, away', and – once again – *kryptos*, 'cryptic, hidden') had only connotations of secretiveness and concealment, even though the church soon shifted this towards ideas of fraudulence and fakery. But let us not forget that, when it comes to their authorship, each of the gospels is actually apocryphal, given that all were written by anonymous individuals and signed with other people's names. And as for texts dictated by supernatural entities, each of these is a put-up job. It is only the passage of time that has conferred on them at least one condition that allows for authenticity to be spoken of – that is, the fact that they are now vestiges of history.

During those first centuries of Christianity, other objects also began to appear: relics. In their zeal for anything that would confer legitimacy, the prelates initiated a stockpiling phase whose aim was not tremendously honourable: to amass any segment or snippet of the bodies of any saints, however small, as well as any garment or effect that had come into contact with one of those bodies. These relics were something that could then be venerated, but it wouldn't be long before they took on a commercial value. What were probably the first large-scale forgeries in history then followed. To the forgers, the religious aspect took a backseat; commercial value was all. You had pilgrims and mercers who made a living purely from these transactions. There were entire monasteries dedicated to the production and export of relics. The liturgy began to include the blessed oil that had been used inside lamps from Jerusalem's holy places and at the tombs of saints and martyrs. And these holy oils then began to multiply. Accordingly, there were military Christian orders, such as the Knights Templar, that started out as armed guards when relics were being transported and ended up making the trade in relics throughout the Mediterranean their principal source of finance; they distributed and sold vials of holy oil in their thousands, along with pieces of the crown of thorns and fragments of the true cross. In the Middle Ages, all those hundreds of years after the crucifixion, there was such a proliferation of supposedly authentic chunks of the true cross that Calvin, in his 1543 *Treatise on Relics*, went as far as saying that 'if one were to accept all such claims, one would have enough wood to fill up a ship's cargo hold. The Gospel tells us that it was possible for a man to carry the cross. It is pure effrontery to fill the Earth with enough fragments of wood that even three hundred men could not carry them.'

The crucifixion nails, of which there would have been no more than three – four, according to the most generous theories – reproduced just like the wood of the cross. There are more than a dozen holy grails from which Christ drank at the last supper. In Italy, France and Spain alone, there are seventeen holy shrouds. The breastmilk with which the Virgin Mary nursed her son became so widespread throughout the churches and convents of the Middle Ages that one has to wonder who it was that extracted such huge amounts of that liquid, and under what circumstances.

Sixty-two fingers of John the Baptist have been counted. On top of which, based on the number of churches with his complete skull on display – the authenticated relic of his complete skull – it turns out he was a saint with precisely eighteen heads.

The demand for relics became so huge it was difficult to keep up. To make the business truly lucrative, as well as pieces linked to well-known biblical characters, people began trading in more minor ones – easier to produce, harder to verify: the filings from the nails of any saint who happened to have been crucified; soil from any grave deemed holy; scraps of cloths from the habits worn by martyrs; the hair, teeth and nail clippings belonging to the least beatus. The only possible equivalent of counterfeiting on this sort of scale in modern times is the manufacture of fake designer handbags, sunglasses, perfumes and clothes – ubiquitous in shopping centres, market stalls and flea markets.

But, between these bookends, many other seams opened up in the history of commercially motivated forgeries. For one, almost as soon as it became a feature of society, money itself began to be forged. To begin with, since the coins themselves had value depending on the metal from which they were made, all one needed to do was to weigh them to see whether they had been forged using baser metals, or indeed whether someone had filed them down to collect the shavings. It wasn't long ago that people would still bite coins to see if they would bend or not. With the appearance of banknotes and modern technologies, the forgery process has become increasingly sophisticated, though this hasn't prevented nearly a million fake banknotes continuing to circulate internationally every year. In the same way, ever since they came into existence, titles of nobility and property deeds, contracts, financial guarantees, endorsement letters, witness statements and membership cards have also been falsified. And, likewise, as certain books came to be worth more – because they were rare, unique or particularly antique – the task of the copyist was also gradually replaced by that of the forger, who produced replica codices, illuminated manuscripts and incunabula dating back to the dawn of the printing press. Specialist collectors and bibliophiles have paid genuine fortunes for certain volumes. And, on occasion, forgeries have been so singular as to become more valuable than the originals.

Something similar has happened in art forgery, another rich seam for those looking to make money from counterfeiting. Some say that the celebrated Hungarian forger Elmyr de Hory – who sold thousands of imitation paintings, and whom Orson Welles played in the 1973 docudrama *Fraud (F for Fake)* – was forced to produce work of lower quality than he was truly able to, so that it would more closely resemble the originals. De Hory even managed to sell a fake Matisse to Harvard's meticulous Fogg Art Museum. And there is no doubt that, if he'd been born in the Renaissance or any other era that had a greater appreciation of art as mimesis, life would have treated him far more kindly. The same goes for Hans van Meergeren, who succeeded in getting a museum in Rotterdam to buy his forged version of Vermeer's *Supper at Emmaus*. But both happened to be born with the Second World War on the horizon. De Hory was arrested by the Nazis for being Jewish and a homosexual; he had a leg broken in the interrogation by the Gestapo, though he later escaped from the hospital. After years as a wanted man, being condemned across the world and exploited by other forgers who passed on to him small fractions of the millions they made on his work, he would end up committing suicide. Meanwhile, chance saw to it that the founder of the Gestapo, Hermann Göring, would buy one of Van Meergeren's Vermeers for US$850,000. Then, when the war was over, Van Meergeren was thrown in jail by his own compatriots, accused of handing over Dutch national heritage to the Germans; he was compelled to admit that it was in fact nothing more than one of the many forgeries by his own hand. And yet none of the art experts called upon in his trial would agree with him: according to them, these paintings were the genuine originals. Van Meergeren's only hope to get off the hook as a collaborator and avoid the death penalty was then to paint a new Vermeer in front of a live audience. What he didn't imagine, when he admitted his guilt on counts of fraud – which would still mean prison – was that his heart would not stand up to the whole thing.

And yet none of these art forgeries had what could properly be called an artistic purpose – they were merely a way of earning a living for people who never had the good fortune to make it as artists. A Greek sculpture – or one sold as such though it actually isn't – is still an attempt to swindle people out of money, even if the person who made it was Michelangelo. In fact, before his *Cupid Sleeping* was bought by Cardinal Raffaele Riario, Michelangelo had followed the advice given to him by Lorenzo di Pierfrancesco de Médicis: 'If you can make it look like it's been lying in the soil for a long time', he said, 'I could send it to Rome, where it will be taken for something ancient, and it would fetch a far better price.'

And so Michelangelo did. He distressed the piece, before burying it for a time, and the cardinal would end up buying it for something in the region of 200 ducats. The dealer responsible for the sale, however, sent only 30 ducats to

Michelangelo: he took the rest as commission, having learnt that the piece was fake. It mattered not at all that the transaction would, in time, ultimately end up adding to the Vatican's already huge piles of wealth.

Throughout the Second World War, with postmodernity just around the corner, falsifications in the arena of armed conflict went far beyond the fabrication of inflatable tank squadrons, artillery and planes, and were not restricted to the efforts of the Allies; their opponents came up with hundreds of their own. Ten of thousands, in fact, if we take into account the reams of forged documents necessitated by espionage and counter-espionage activities. Nor is it possible to say that the Third Reich was less imaginative on this count than the Allied powers.[1] Far from it. The Germans even went as far as forging money as a war tactic, rather than for personal gain. Among the Nazis' many secret plans to defeat their opponents was Operation Bernhardt, the idea of which was to make the British economy collapse by flooding it with £300 million in counterfeit £5, £10, £20 and £50 notes. This operation, which would have provided funds to continue defraying the German war

[1] We should not forget that, as it happens, in 1933 they created the Ministry of Propaganda, which Joseph Goebbels would succeed in turning into a machine precisely for creating forgeries and altering the truth. There would soon be replicas of this organization in the shape of the Portuguese Ministry for National Propaganda (created in 1933), Italy's Ministry for Popular Culture (1937) and Spain's Ministry for Popular Education (1941), and it would provide the primary inspiration for George Orwell's Ministry of Truth. It's also true that, though the vast majority of the public are still unaware of the fact, the author of *1984*'s main source for illustrating the mechanisms of censorship and how politically motivated lies could be deployed was his experience of working at the BBC. It was no coincidence that the most terrifying space in the entire novel, in which torture would be meted out to crush independent thought, had the same name as his office at work: Room 101.

effort while simultaneously provoking economic chaos in Great Britain, was the first time in history that a nation state applied its technical capacities to the forgery of paper money. The resultant copies were of such high quality that, although it didn't take long for the manoeuvre to be found out, the British government had no choice but to prevent word of the attack getting out and to allow the fake notes introduced by then to go on being used; they would remain in circulation for years. The Bank of England undertook a gradual process of changing the designs on the officially sanctioned currency, and retaining the fake banknotes – which, when brought to auction in later years, went on to sell for far more than their nominal values.

Counterfeiting with military aims in mind is in a very similar realm, finally, to politically motivated counterfeiting. When it comes to the trumped-up documents accusing Iraq of having weapons of mass destruction, were these militarily motivated, or rather to do with political justification both at home and in the eyes of the international community? Governments that constantly resort to 'alternative facts' and media manipulation often do so, in the case of democracies, because they want to justify their conduct either to the polity or to their political rivals, while, in the case of dictatorships, it is about giving coherency and consistency to the larger lie they are selling to their subjects. But, more than for anything else, all manner of spurious practices – from the little white lies to the barefaced ones, and from ancient times to our contemporary moment – have been used in the construction of national identities. All human beings and all peoples hoping to build a shared identity have always been obsessed with rewriting history. And there is no culture anywhere on earth that does not base itself on fictitious legends and falsehoods.

The first national epics, like *Gilgamesh* or Homer's *Iliad*, mixed together fantastical elements with supposed historical events. The mediaeval *chansons de geste*, like *Beowulf* in England, *The Song of the Nibelungs* in Germany, and *The Poem of the Cid* in Spain, used lying to sing the praises of heroic feats that could serve as a model for their societies. Not until the invention of nationalist ideologies at the end of the eighteenth century would this practice go into a fatal sort of overdrive. From the Industrial Revolution onwards, we see the dominant political and economic powers begin to invent imaginary communities to serve their own interests better. The expansion of the printing press would be exploited in order to rewrite history as those in power saw fit, accentuating whichever differences best served them – whether racial, linguistic, religious or to do with anything else; to recuperate hitherto overlooked heroes of the past; to rejig national events, hymns and myths; and above all to give shape to a raft of unpardonable offences. Nationalist ideology always entails the need for the forging of documents and images.[2] These foundational records will later be backed up by a new and ever-expanding bibliography, created to serve the interests of their respective

[2] Perhaps one of the earliest and most famous photographic manipulations with nationalistic aims belongs to the history of the USSR (the historiographic efforts of which are among the most eventful in the twentieth century, given the extremity of the manipulation, rewriting and counterfeiting involved). The photo in question was taken on 5 May 1920, during an address by Lenin to the Soviet troops outside Moscow's Bolshoi Theatre. Leon Trotsky originally appears next to the speaking podium. However, after Stalin's ascent to power, Trotsky became a 'non-person': a person whose name, like that of most of the revolutionary leaders, could not be mentioned, and whose image was not allowed to feature in any printed matter whatsoever. And, in effect – possibly by dint of scalpel and airbrush – Trotsky ended up being expunged from the photo.

nationalisms. But the important thing is that the slights on which enmities are based should remain present and alive, with attendant (bogus) documentation. Nationalist ideologies were the seed for the First World War; were crucial in the rise of the various early- to mid-twentieth-century fascisms, as well as Stalinism; and were the cause of the Second World War and all the wars of independence. They can also, when taken together with economic interests and religious fervour, explain virtually all the armed conflicts that have ever taken place. Looking at nationalisms around the world, we see at least four shared themes: they make the political class more powerful; they add to the wealth of the dominant economic class, and further impoverish the middle and working classes; they exacerbate division and dislike between neighbours; and they strike the most distant foreigners as incomprehensible, frivolous or superficial.

Those persuaded by nationalist rhetoric, regardless of which flag it pertains to, are people who have a deep desire to see their beliefs confirmed. And they will adopt any arguments they deem favourable to their cause, even if they have not taken the time to analyse them and know nothing of their provenance. Therefore, victims of this chimera are especially susceptible to manipulation and counterfeiting.

Consequently, in a world where it is increasingly difficult to believe what we see with our own eyes, the only way to avoid the fallacies of identity is to take a step back. And try to see things with the dispassionate view of a foreign observer.

Or, better still, accept it as a given that everybody lies.

ART AS FABRICATION

When, in full awareness that all is deception, we get swept along because we actually just want to be swept along, art arises.

The artist is a virtuoso of storytelling, expert in the deployment of symbols and metaphors. So, no one is better equipped to speak about reality – not to try to alter it to her advantage, not to break it, not to dissect it to control the way it functions, but to speak about it.

Just like mythical and religious thinking, creativity is simply another accidental upshot of the evolutionary trait that is our intelligence. But artists give themselves up to lying so completely that, by their very recognition that everything they do is fiction, they become the least feigning of all.

Like every human being, from the moment they attempt to represent reality, they are fabricating something. Through the primary mental representation, and through the subsequent metaphorical leap to the work. However, works of art differentiate themselves from all other falsifications in that the work is an end in itself. When artists hold their hands up to the falsehood, they confer unprecedented independence and autonomy on the work. Only if the creative intention deviates from such an approach, seeking instead a different benefit – artists who plagiarize others for profit, artists who imitate others in an attempt to assume the same social standing as them, artists who put their talent at the disposal of a political regime, artists who sell themselves – can we speak of a fabrication like any other.

Artists, too, who forget they are involved in deceiving people, and believe their work equally as real as – if not more real than – that which it represents, will have moved into the realm of self-deceit and will thereby distort what art really is. Reality is one big lie. Art is a lie on top of a lie. And the artist must remain constantly aware of being a liar who lies for the sake of lying, rather than for their own sake.

The temptation to reproduce or improve upon reality has for centuries been a trap for artists, and even more so given that art has above all been understood as mimesis, since the first bison was depicted on a cave wall right through to the Renaissance. In Aristotle's *Poetics*, it was already being asserted that the arts all consist of imitation and are distinguished only by the objects they imitate and their means of doing so. However, this definition of art as copying has often given rise to misunderstandings. There is the well-known and often cited episode of the painters Zeuxis and Parrasio from the fifth century BC, who, according to Pliny the Elder, had a competition to establish who was the better artist. The grapes painted by Zeuxis were so real that, when the painting was put on show, the birds fluttered down from the nearby trees to peck at them.

'What are you waiting for? Let's see yours', said Zeuxis, seeing his rival making no move to pull back the curtain covering his canvas.

When he went to do it himself, he was forced to recognize Parrasio as the winner: with his grapes, he had managed to trick only a group of silly birds, whereas, with his brilliantly realized curtain, his rival had tricked a fellow artist.

To understand the art object as a simple mimetic exercise, like a special capacity for faithfully reproducing a certain model, is to reduce it to the same level as handicrafts. Yet this has been the predominant focus for most of human history. It is true that numerous categories have been folded in to mitigate the definition's lack of range, like those of beauty, tragedy, the sublime, pathos, irony and comedy. And, above all of these, beauty; beauty more than anything. Nonetheless, every one of these categories – including, of course, the idea of beauty – is completely subjective. In the best cases, transcendentally subjective. But they depend on the human subject projecting them, and are therefore either fleeting lies, when they adhere to certain fashions or the caprice of taste, or a priori and biological, when they are imposed by our species' modes of perception and understanding.

Throughout this long historic interval, the traditional artist was subject to the double tyranny of imitation and beauty, with the innumerable limitations each imposes on the creative act. They had no choice but to obey the universal injunction to make reality more beautiful than it was, or to create a second-order reality even more beautiful than the first. Within this rather narrow conception, art depended not only on the artist's subjective intention, talent and perception, but on the prevailing idea of beauty in the time and culture in which they happened to be operating.

Liberation from the tyranny of beauty did not come until the twentieth century, with the emergence of the avant-gardists. It was only in modern times that people began to understand that art doesn't have to be beautiful. Until this moment, people didn't realize that art need not be limited to the imitation of reality. What is more, imitation is one of the most elemental forms of fabrication, which hardly makes for an original contribution, nor a genuine creative challenge. Of course, by the time we get to Van Gogh's sunflowers, we're already looking at something not merely seeking to mimic the world beyond the canvas, but Cubism's explosive arrival was a far greater rupture. The principal idea with Cubism is to demonstrate a brazen opposition to the classical idea of beauty, which is why it even suppresses the colour and emotion seen in the Impressionists. In the same way, Dadaism will look to break with the dominion of logic, while at the same time introducing into poetry and sculpture all manner of unconventional materials that make for a whole new set of expressive possibilities.

The avant-garde failed to eliminate art's governing norms and fictions, precisely because it is these fictions that make art possible. Nonetheless, its frontal attack on the old conventions meant an unprecedented normative expansion, one that liberated the human imagination in previously impossible ways. The arts of the twentieth century have ventured down untrodden paths, and the creative mechanisms involved in the process have never been so numerous. Purely mimetic works go on being produced to this day, granted, but they have lost their privileged status as far as the critical conversation goes, and the audiences that still choose them only do so if unaware of these changes.

To the contemporary artist, everything now seems possible.

However, the discovery of the absence of aesthetic limitations does not mean the norms just disappear. Far from it. This is because, on the one hand, the artist always belongs to a historical context; even now, the artist coexists with a cluster of lies and illusions to which she is subject, and which will one day dissipate with the emergence of a new paradigm. And, on the other, because the only things distinguishing the art object from any other object created by humans – domestic, handcrafted, industrial, commercial – are the very norms and the aggregate of theories that cluster around it. The object in itself, stripped of all these fictions, is not art; it requires an artistic community that accredits it as such. It requires a critical corpus to pick it out, to reflect on it, to explain why in this particular moment and historical context it constitutes art, and which of its qualities make it better or worse than other works. Art, therefore, can never do without the human actions that surround it: the artist's intentions, the interpretation of the reader or audience, critical vindication. It needs a framework of reception, even though this is a far broader thing in the present day, and previously unconsidered factors have entered the equation.

And the artist's awareness of the creative process itself now counts among the factors seen as determining the artistic act. Her awareness that she is making art and making use of fabrication to that end. Her intention being artistic rather than merely commercial – the latter being what drives somebody making actual urinals, for example. Her wish to create illusions; the artist takes pleasure in creating fictions in full knowledge that they are fictions. And that goes for those at whom the work is aimed; they too are capable of taking pleasure in the lie. Anyone faced with a work of conceptual art knows that they are being drawn into a game of reinterpretation and construction about what is real, that this isn't a portrait or a still life. The voracious consumer of extreme violence at the movies cannot, in the vast majority of cases, avoid looking away when confronted with a similar situation in real life, and will change channel when a news item comes on showing people *actually* dying. Their capacity for aesthetic pleasure distinguishes between what is and what isn't fiction.

Postmodernity itself is, to a large extent, a reflection on this awareness of the lie. The classical artist made things by way of metaphor. The postmodern artist constructs a metaphor about the metaphor. And is aware of the metaphorical, circumstantial, fictive and meta-fictive conditions of this act. Postmodernity undoubtedly entailed a giant qualitative leap in the evolution of our cultural activities. Even if its great problem is that it remains dazzled by its own discovery: the metaphor for the metaphor for the metaphor. And that it appears unable to find a way out of its own self-pleasuring loop.

A wider perspective will be necessary, one still invisible to the artist's contemporaries, in order to inaugurate a new period in which we can take art to another level. Another level for us, at least. Because art will always be a human act, by and for humans. In the eyes of nature – to the birds, to the hurricane sweeping through the ruins, to whatever the numen may be, or the thing in itself – an artwork is in no way different from any other artefact. It could only be so if a divinity existed in our image that could understand all the things we get up to. Objects cannot in themselves be different from or better than others. Artworks can only be superior for the community for which they were created. It is the art world itself – made up of the makers, the gallery owners, dealers, experts and critics – that invents the norms governing the artistic act. Art will be whatever they happen to say art is, and their decree will hold a specific weight for the rest of society. Once the dictatorships of beauty and mimesis have been overthrown, and all the other limitations of the aesthetic canon quashed, the only thing that can confer such a status on the work is the judgement of the agents involved. The appraisal of the different actors in the game, and the efficiency of the critical apparatus generated around every author and every work.

LITERATURE AS FABRICATION

The idea of fabrication, being as it is inextricable from art, has also been present in the history of literature since its beginnings.

The mechanisms of verisimilitude – when understood as the facets of the work intended to mitigate the falseness of the tale – are intrinsic in every narrative act, whether oral or written. This is because the function of the poet will not be to recount events that have happened, but rather, as Aristotle also stated in *Poetics*, to recount the events that *could* happen, and to do so in a believable way. Meanwhile, we cannot forget that in the classical Greco-Latin world, where artistic creation was understood as a mimetic activity, absolute originality was both an impossible aspiration and, often, not one to be desired. Certain thinkers – Seneca among them – saw the literary tradition as a shared store for all writers, from which they could take, copy or transform whatever they liked, and the advice here was to avoid quoting explicitly and to hide whatever material had been appropriated. And the awareness of the game, the artifice and the aesthetics of fabrication would only intensify over the centuries.

Finally, there will be Borges, with his view that all literature is plagiarism.

Imagination is combination and, to a large extent, the

advances in and development of literature have come about through intertextuality – texts communicating between one another – and it is this that will allow for a cumulative growth. Writers will communicate with other writers, via their works and via an endless number of techniques that relate to plagiarism but are purely and essentially literary: imitation, quotation, collage, mirroring, fakes and remakes. No writer will be ashamed to make use of these resources – rather, these glances in the direction of other works will be interpreted as homage, and the mutations and alterations as nothing but new possibilities in the game. This is why, ever since antiquity, there has always been an abundance of manuscripts recounting imaginary journeys to other continents or to the moon. Or bestiaries describing in great detail completely made-up creatures. Or spurious quotations from non-existent books, which function as red herrings or invitations to go on imagining limitlessly inside the interminable labyrinth. In *Gargantua and Pantagruel* (1532–64), Rabelais makes reference to more than 150 imaginary works. Jonathan Swift, Nabokov, H. P. Lovecraft, Borges and Stanisław Lem are also keen on adding to the ranks of this rare species of fictitious book.

Jorge Luis Borges wrote one short story, 'The Approach to Al-Mu'tasim', in the form of a review of a non-existent novel that had even his friends fooled for years. And the previously mentioned 'Tlön, Uqbar, Orbis Tertius', as well as 'An Examination of the Work of Herbert Quain', repeat the trick of analysing texts that never existed, which ultimately brings us to the idea that fabrication can be an effective mode for creating – or recreating – the world. In 'Pierre Menard, Author of the Quixote', Borges ponders the possibility of a copy, spontaneously created in a different historical context, being at the same time identical to and different from the original: 'Cervantes' text and Menard's are verbally identical, but the second is almost infinitely richer.'

The creative possibilities of adulteration and distortion are endless. The Polish writer Stanisław Lem also came up with a curious library of imaginary books, composed of four volumes: *A Perfect Vacuum* (1971), *Imaginary Magnitude* (1973), *Golem XIV* (1981) and *Provocation* (1982). In these, amid an avalanche of apparently scientific facts that conjure the sensation of verisimilitude, Lem pieces together a structure of prologues, reviews, compendiums and pastiches that will delight any reader wishing to learn how to get lost.

But, even if we stretch imposture to its full extent, even to the point of altering the name or identity of the author itself, new facets in the artistic event will continue appearing and unfolding. So, it is possible for a writer not only to hide their name behind a pseudonym, but, by the same process of substitution, to come up with a heteronym – that is, an invented character, with their own personality and apparent autonomy, whose principal function will be to put their name to certain works by the author. This would be the case with Monsieur Teste, a character conceived by Paul Valéry 'at a period when I was drunk on my own will and subject to strange excesses of consciousness of my self'. And it was the same with Honorio Bustos Domecq, an author created by Borges and Adolfo Bioy Casares, whose name would go on four of their collaborative books and whom they also gave his own biography. Antonio Machado came up with no less than thirty-three heteronyms, of which the Professor in Rhetoric Juan de Mairena, and the poet, philosopher and student of Mairena,

Abel Martín – both Sevillians – came to be the most well known. The Portuguese Fernando Pessoa managed to keep no less than seventy-two heteronyms in the air, from the renowned Alberto Caeiro, Álvaro Campos, Bernardo Soares and Ricardo Reis to lesser offshoots such as Thomas Crosse and Pero Botelho.

And if an author wishes to falsify their own person, this is also an option. On one hand, the techniques of autofiction necessarily imply a kind of distortion and fabrication of the self, which are gradually dissolved into the story to the point where they melt into an indistinguishable whole: equal parts reality and fiction. And, on the other, writers will always have the chance to create a character for themselves in every interview they give, in which they can go on being more split, more distant from their private selves.

But is it really true to say that anything goes? Are there no limits to the literary methods of deceit? Yes, of course there are – at least in terms of cleaving to the artistic phenomenon. Avellaneda's *Quixote*, for instance – *A Continuation of the History and Adventures of the Renowned Don Quixote de la Mancha*, by one Alonso Fernández de Avellaneda – is a substantially different case from those we have discussed. Quite aside from any literary attributes or qualities of its own, from the moment it sought, by rushing to be printed in 1614, to take over someone else's unfinished project, exploited the success of the authentic first part, and was laid bare as retaliation for something Cervantes had done, it assumed a position outside of the ambit of literature. The dividing line may be diffuse, in the sense that authorial self-interest is a factor in both, but there is still a moment when deceit for artistic purposes can tip over into fraud. In the same way, many of the instances of plagiarism in recent years have been judged in court, rather than by critical consensus.[1]

The intentions change, the judges change. Because there are lies, and then there are lies.

However, both in art in general and in literature in particular, due partly to all the fictional possibilities both bring with them, it will sometimes be difficult to distinguish between major and minor lies, between a sublime kind of deceit and mere swindling. Lying is the most distinctive sign of intelligence, but its complexity in the present day seems to have brought us to the limit of our capacity for mystification. Art, as we have seen, is context-dependent, so we also need to bear in mind that the great fictions of art not only have to exist alongside so many other inferior lies, they also sometimes use them for a leg up. From the moment in which the validation criteria of the artwork depend on the artistic community itself, the creator will be compelled to enter the reputation-building circuits and the game of prestige. At which point, farcical pretence,

[1] Among the most widely reported cases are those of Manuel Vázquez Montalbán, found guilty of plagiarizing a translation; Alfredo Brye Echenique, found guilty of plagiarizing sixteen articles from newspapers; Nobel Prize-winner Camilo José Cela, found guilty by courts in Barcelona of appropriating the contents of a different novel that had been entered for a prize, the Premio Planeta, that Cela went on to win; Lucía Etxebarria, found guilty of plagiarizing the work of Antonio Colinas, and accused on several other counts; Arturo Pérez-Reverte, who, at the time of writing, has been found guilty by the Audiencia Provincial Courts in Madrid, in spite of three previous rulings in his favour. One quite different case – in its goals and motivations – is *El Hacedor (de Borges), Remake* (The Maker (by Borges), Remake) by Agustín Fernández-Mallo, which was never accused of being plagiaristic; however, Borges's widow and legatee, María Kodama, in a quite incredible show of ignorance regarding the body of work left in her care, as well as of the way literature functions, demanded that this intertextual homage be withdrawn from all bookshops.

rhetoric, intrigue, slander, boastfulness and other schemes come into play once more.

The contributing factors in the consecration of an author are so many and so diverse that we inevitably begin to feel that the entire process is governed by pure chance.

Even so, we know that certain universal works of art have transcended their time and culture, and this gives us a feeling that a sort of justice does exist. That time does put things in their rightful place. The hope for posterity. But this is no more than an old desire, whatever qualities we attribute to these works; critics and art philosophers alike will be hard pressed to find qualities completely independent of the canons of human communities that designate them as artistic.

And for every author that time rescues, thousands are unjustly forgotten.[2]

---

[2] It would be impossible to list the thousands of writers whose names have not come down to our current day, or whose work was destroyed in centuries past. But, to mention a handful whose works we still do have, can we really say that history has given the Argentinian writer Macedonio Fernández his proper dues? What about the Peruvian Julio Ramón Ribeyro? The Mexican Rafael Bernal? The Uruguayan Mario Levrero? And in Spain, have we really done justice to the superlative Álvaro Cunqueiro, Rafael Dieste, Wenceslao Fernández Flórez or Joan Perucho?

Has history really acted as it should with writers such as Murasaki Shikibu, author of the first known novel in the history of literature? How about María de Zayas from the Spanish Golden Age, who wrote the Spanish *Decameron*? Or Amandine Aurore Lucile Dupin, who was forced to write under the male pen name George Sand to avoid being considered a minor artist? Has the canon made space for the likes of Elizabeth von Arnim, Concha Espina, Grazia Deledda, Willa Cather, Mary MacLane, Isak Dinesen, Vicki Baum, Dorothy Parker, Florbela Espanca, Rosa Chacel, Zelda Fitzgerald, Nina Berbérova, María Teresa León, Ernestina de Champourcín, Christina Stead, María Virginia Estenssoro, Irène Némirovsky, Irmgard Keun, Mercè Rodoreda, Jean Stafford, Elena Garro, Natalia Ginzburg, Shirley Jackson, Estrella Alfon, Mavis Gallant, Taeko Kōno, Elizabeth Hardwick, Amparo

As we have said: there is no justice in art, and history does not give everyone their proper dues.

In any case, what kind of strange thing could posterity be in a world that, up to the present moment, has been pure facade?

Dávila, Maria Gabriela Llansol, Brigitte Reimann, Joan Didion, Agota Kristof, Alejandra Pizarnik, Edith Pearlman, Lucia Berlin, Hebe Uhart, Joanna Russ, Angela Carter, Verity Bargate, Ama Ata Aidoo, Joy Williams or Adelaida García Morales . . .?

THE MASTERS OF SCEPTICISM

And here we are again, esteemed reader, after the long journey. Finally addressing the state of the matter in question during our present moment.

I therefore think it opportune, before we consider our way of being in the world today, to give a final overview of how we got from Descartes to where we now find ourselves. The reality we left outside when we were trapped within the thinking subject was rigid, unmovable and unequivocal. Whereas what we see unfolding around us now seems far more uncertain, the reflection of a conjectural and fluctuating reality. But what are the principal changes that have brought us to this precise situation?

Paul Ricoeur, in *Freud and Philosophy: An Essay on Interpretation* (1965), was the first to call Marx, Nietzsche and Freud the three 'masters of scepticism'. It was they, in his account, who unmasked the old truths, they who more than anyone wrought the change that placed the crisis of modern philosophy in full view and denounced the lie of consciousness. Marx did this by signalling ideology and economic interests as chimeras reflecting an inverted awareness of the world. Nietzsche, by demolishing the concept of truth itself and turning moral values into something else entirely. And Freud, by relegating consciousness and reason to a lower rung, and by giving irrationality back its true primordial place. The triple-unmasking to which Ricoeur alluded was, however, not nearly as simple as that, but rather part of a far wider movement. A small multitude of thinkers, researchers and scientists from the second half of the nineteenth century and first half of the twentieth, without necessarily having any interaction, and in most cases without knowing one another's work, applied themselves to this self-same cause. During this time, virtually all disciplines underwent the same crisis and the same rebuilding process. As can only occur in a species connected by an invisible structure, by the tangled mesh of culture, all the fields and areas of our understanding were hit by a similar seismic shock, because of which truth, man and reason were repeatedly toppled. Our fictional dimension makes us akin to an insect colony. And humanity, like the superorganism that it is, had reached the moment of transformation.

It would be excessive to give a detailed account here of our culture's complex process of change in respect of its vision of itself. I will therefore limit myself to a brief overview of the chief areas of intellectual enquiry involved, to give us at least something of an idea about how the world caved in before being reborn in the shape we now know it.

It was 1845 when, not only in the ambit of philosophy, but also in those of economics and political science, an unexpected and intense shockwave was about to hit: *The German Ideology* was in gestation, though it would still be several decades before it saw the light of day. In that 500-page tome – a collaboration with Engels – Karl Marx would claim that reality as it had been conceived of until then was nothing but an ideological superstructure, a mirage projected by a self-interested minority. Marx would invite his fellow citizens to break through this society-generated illusion; to see beyond the veil of moral, aesthetic and religious values imposed by the few; and to take a new sounding of reality for themselves. The reality Marx sees is different from that seen by any other philosopher – philosophers who, with that work, he would begin to surpass. It is not a reality of mere relations between abstract concepts, composed of categories, prejudices or ideologies, but rather a reality that both is beyond reason and has an effective existence in the world. For the founder of historical materialism, the irrational-material is not only more real than the rational, it is the true motor of the world.

Not long afterwards, in 1859, Charles Darwin would publish a highly anticipated book, whose entire first print run would sell out within a day of being on sale: *On the Origin of Species*, a work destined irrevocably to displace man from the centre of creation. The repercussions of Darwin's evolutionary theory were devastating to established mythical conceptions of the world, and definitively unmasked all the origin stories (for which, read 'lies') that had been with us for centuries. Nonetheless, his idea of natural selection would also have innumerable knock-on effects in areas quite distinct from biology, such as sociology, economics, the philosophy of science and even cognitive epistemology.

At the time, a young and unpredictable Friedrich Nietzsche was beginning to publish, meaning a new cataclysm was just around the corner. When *On Truth and Lies in a Nonmoral Sense* appeared in 1873, it would prove the greatest blow to the heart of the long-standing paradigm of reality, its target being the very foundations of the notion of truth. For Nietzsche, as we have seen, the truth is only something conjured up by the weak, who are afraid to be truly alive – an invention on the part of Socrates, Plato and the Judaeo-Christians to lock man up in the narrow cell of reason and separate him from his passions. The new truth will be no more than a kind of error without which a certain species of living beings – us – could not survive. By exalting lies in a nonmoral sense, Nietzsche will glorify fictions to the point of making them indispensable, regulatory elements in the psychic, moral, social and cognitive life of human beings, as well as inserting himself into an underappreciated philosophical current, one usually referred to as Fictionalism.[1] Human intelligence, within the Nietzschean

[1] Jeremy Bentham (1748–1832) can almost certainly be counted as the founder of Fictionalism. For him, every description of the world that does not represent a real or perceptible thing is a fiction, although he distinguishes between 'fabulous entities', like Prince Hamlet or a centaur, and 'fictitious entities', like Kant's categories, human rights and the social contract. The Italian Giovanni Marchesini would also follow this line of thinking, with the view, expressed in *Le finzioni dell'anima* (The Illusion of the Soul, 1905), that moral values are fictions projected by consciousness, but that they should nonetheless not be considered simple hallucinations, due to the fact that they function as effective regulators on our spiritual and moral life. And finally – though more influenced by Nietzsche than by Marchesini – the German Hans Vaihinger would contribute to this strain of thought with *Philosophie des Als Ob* (The Philosophy of 'As If'), which was published in 1911. For Vaihinger, not all terms with a fictional connotation may be reduced to the same category of fiction; thus, the *principium* is a departure point; the *sumptio*, a simple admission of something expressed in a statement; the *suppositio*, the next level of presumption; the *conjectura* is at the level of hypothesis; the *praesumptio* is a presupposition in the moral sense; the *fictio*, the product of the creative imagination, etc. Consequently, although it cannot be said that fictions *are*, neither can it be said that they *are not*. The fictions understood in this way are quasi-concepts that denote quasi-things (electrons and protons in physics, for example, or the quasi-crime in law) and, though they do not permit knowledge of the underlying reality of the world, they do provide human beings with the possibility of constructing systems of thought and behaviour 'as if' the world fitted their models. For each of these three authors, fictions may at times consist of mere falsehoods, but they may also at others result in useful opportunities to come to provisionally valid conclusions, which in turn may lead us to further discoveries.

view of things, consists of nothing more than the art of feigning.

Nonetheless, just a few decades on, there will be a third broadside for religion and Christianity to withstand, with the publication of *The Joyous Science* (1882) and *Thus Spake Zarathustra* (1883–5). In these, nothing less than the death of God was diagnosed. Without that death, man could never be freed from the moral Christian code, which, with its concept of guilt, was keeping him in chains, and neither could the Superman come into being. Not content with this, to cap the entrance to this new human phase, Nietzsche also proposed, in *Beyond Good and Evil* (1886) and *The Genealogy of Morals* (1887), the necessity of transforming human values – a complete reconstruction of those values that we allowed to direct our lives and that until that moment had been concomitant with a morality of masters and slaves.

Ferdinand de Saussure would also play a part in our new scepticism about reality – increasingly nothing more than a construct of language – with his *Course in General Linguistics* (1913). The father of linguistic structuralism would introduce a profound gap between signifier and signified – one that would mean we were permanently separated from things in themselves. In Saussurean theory, the link between signified and signifier is arbitrary, speech is no more than an accident of language, and the study of deep structures can only be synchronic rather than diachronic: we may analyse the functioning of language in a specific historical context, but any study of its evolution over time will only lead to superficial conclusions.

In the same way, many of Sigmund Freud's principal works – from *The Interpretation of Dreams* (1900) to *The Ego and the Id* (1923) – would contribute to deposing the self from its position at the centre of both the world and human knowledge, placing the murky unconscious at the forefront of all our actions. But, at this advanced stage, what remains standing after Freud? In a scenario like our reality, already so debilitated, there is very little that can withstand the battering of psychoanalysis. On top of everything, any human action must now be considered to have certain hidden, deeper purposes, dictated by our irrational part, by the unconscious, by desire. Purposes that nobody, not even the subject herself, knows, because they have been disguised by the repressive impulse. What one thinks about one's own actions has ceased to be of much importance. There is some covert thing directing the world from the shadows. Once again, the self and our supposing identity are a fiction, within a society far stranger and more chaotic than we had imagined.

It took barely 100 years of attacks and critiques for the ironclad reality of the Middle Ages – which had done what it could to hold off the arrival of modernity – to vanish without trace. The foundations of our convictions came tumbling down and we were perplexed to discover that reality in its entirety was no more than a false, prettified construct. We suddenly comprehended that, in all probability, we were projecting models of order on to the world – taking them for genuine principles and laws, when those principles could just as well be completely different or simply not exist.

And these same debacles would go on happening in all other realms of humanity. That which had occurred in philosophy, religion, politics, morality, economics, biology, linguistics and psychology would repeat in every other field. Within the movement of structuralism itself, Lévi-Strauss would adapt Saussure's theories to anthropology, with his view that social phenomena – myths, rituals, art, personal relationships – can be considered systems of symbols, and furthermore revealing that human thought in the Neolithic times was structured in exactly the same way as modern scientific analysis. Roland Barthes, another of the structuralists, would bring this same transformation to the literary act, and it would be his friend, the philosopher Jacques Derrida, who would inaugurate deconstructionism, which sought to understand not what the text is saying but what it is referring to without actually saying it, attempting to probe the depths of metaphor, suggestion and fiction, making it possible even to disagree radically with an author's interpretation of their own work. Foucault knocked sanity off its pedestal with his studies on normalization, which added up to the idea that normality is no more than a consensus constructed upon an idealization of conduct (the discourses around madness, illness, delinquency and sexuality are recent inventions). In physics, Einstein demolished the Newtonian system with his theory of relativity: the law of universal gravitation that had served us effectively for centuries was no more than a transient belief. And, ten years later, Heisenberg would introduce his uncertainty principle in quantum physics. Meanwhile, the philosophers of science Thomas S. Kuhn and Paul Feyerabend would try to explain how these dismissals of scientific paradigms are possible, and in the process reveal to us science's best-kept secret: it too is a great fashioner of lies, dependent on fraudulent strategies and incapable of guaranteeing one single truth.

THE LIES OF SCIENCE

The idea of science as an unequivocal whole, with all its branches and theories compatible, containing demonstrable, universally valid and everlasting truths, and in which progress is possible, is nothing more than another invention by modern society and its scientific communities. None of these things is so.

And the phrase we are forever hearing – 'it's been scientifically proven' – is nothing but the perfect expression of a new dogma.

Thomas S. Kuhn, a philosopher of science and physics at the University of Harvard, revolutionized everything we thought we knew about science in his 1962 work *The Structure of Scientific Revolutions*. In contrast to Karl Popper with his theory of falsification, which is an attempt to determine how science ought to function in ideal conditions, Kuhn was, rather, to investigate and try to explain the way scientific procedures actually function.

For Kuhn, modern science as we know it always needs to be based on paradigms – that is, sets of conventions that for certain periods of time model the problems and their solutions for the scientific community that takes them as read. And neither does science develop in some ivory tower through the immaculate accumulation of autonomous discoveries and inventions, but rather as part of the overlapping meshwork also comprising all other manifestations of the culture; this is why, should we try to establish the exact moment of any particular discovery, what we always find instead are innumerable partial discoveries and interwoven theories.

When science was still a young discipline, the diversity of competing schools and sub-schools stymied any advance: from antiquity until the seventeenth century, for example, there would be no single accepted theory on the nature of light, and, although the different currents of thought were peopled by scientists who based their knowledge on empirical experiments, nobody who studied optics during that period would have dared to qualify it as a science. Nonetheless, when a paradigm finally emerged – Newtonian optics – all the ensuing research would then use earlier scientific premises as the basis for its later application. From then on, scientists would take the paradigm as a given, which meant not having constantly to reconstruct or justify all the principles in their given field and being able to focus on the piece of research at hand – no need to concern themselves with unresolved problems, which were considered beyond their remit, or the theoretical basis of what they were working on. The story of the scientific development of the paradigm would be a matter for the textbooks; it would be down to them to explain, clearly and concisely, the thrust of the accepted theory, and to illustrate it with idealized observations and experiments, which had little to do with the way in which real observations had been arrived at or experiments carried out. These textbooks, whose job it was to be pedagogical and persuasive, would bend reality to their will and provide for future generations of scientists the sole point of contact with the science itself. People studying the natural sciences in university would come to be taught through nothing but the books created expressly with them in mind, presenting them with everything they needed to know in succinct, precise and systematic form. Confidence in the paradigm would translate, therefore, into far greater efficiency. Scientists would be better prepared for periods of normal development in science, avoiding the kind of heated debates that would hold back other disciplines in the humanities, thereby enabling greater advances in their own. Sure, their sense of the history of science would be completely distorted and – like most people – they would think of it as nothing more than a set of anecdotes concerning just a couple of important questions: who invented or discovered certain things and when, as well as a smattering of information on the erroneous circumstances or superstitions that had prevented these from coming about beforehand.

As if no other option had existed. As if everything in science was predetermined and all that was needed, in order to arrive at the truth, was to follow this one single path.

At the same time, this scientist, so focused in on his own specialism, holed up in his office or lab, and unaware of science's true overall functioning, will be far less well prepared for periods of crisis that will eventually strike.

For, sooner or later, strike they must. This is in spite of the fact that in periods when science is functioning normally, the anomalies that do not fit the prevailing models will go completely unnoticed, and in spite of the fact the scientific community backing the paradigm will go to any lengths to defend it. In reality, in the normal scientific run of things, there is a single point of focus: the resolution of the enigma. The enigmas – as in that class of problems that put to the test the ingenuity or skill required to resolve them – are all that matters. And, as a consequence, just about the only problems that the community will admit as scientific, and that its members will be encouraged to resolve, are those that are expected to have a solution. Whereas other truly pressing problems, like the cure for certain illnesses or achieving lasting peace, are often not considered, by dint of their unsolvability. On top of this, there is a limited number of resolvable problems that a paradigm, and its attendant sensation of progress, can offer. And, sooner or later, it will become impossible to continue covering up the anomalous phenomena. Most of the time, when an anomaly appears that is impossible to ignore, the community will try to adjust the theory to convert the 'abnormal' back into what was expected. But it cannot always be assimilated, and when the number of unexpected transgressions spirals out of control, the crisis hits.

And the crisis will lead to scientific revolution and to the proliferation of other novel paradigms.

These new and competing theoretical visions may ultimately reduce to a single one, though only once a consensus has been reached across science. Then it will be back to a period of scientific business as usual. Whichever paradigm has triumphed after the crisis will initiate a new phase of adaptation, during which all the textbooks will have to be rewritten in favour of its interpretation and to give consistency to its new suppositions. And, given that the future scientists only learn their trade on the basis of up-to-date textbooks, their perception of where their own discipline comes from will be so skewed that they will come to see it as a single, unwavering line.

What remains of this vision of science as a single, monolithic, well-tuned discipline, with utopian points of focus, the carrier of demonstrable truths that promises us endless progress? Very little, if anything. New dogmas. Real science depends on the beliefs of individuals, their capacity to defend them and the arbitrariness in the selection of problems that determine how they are researched.

Not even in moments of normality is the overall impression more encouraging: one need only contemplate all the different fields of science as a whole to comprehend that it is a dilapidated structure, with very little coherence between parts. Otherwise, how can we understand the incompatibility that makes certain paradigms irreconcilable? This lack of conformity between two different, untranslatable systems is manifest not only during the upheaval of a revolution itself, as occurred with Newtonian mechanics and Einstein's theory of relativity. It is also a constant during periods of peaceful coexistence, as we see in the present day with the theory of relativity and quantum physics. The scientists don't have answers for all the grey areas and can't even reflect on these questions or come to a conclusion as to the general direction of travel.

And there is a final element never explicitly tackled by Kuhn, perhaps out of the wish to avoid completely destroying his relationship with the scientific community to which he belonged: the association between science and economic and political power. We cannot ignore the fact that the vast number of research projects undertaken in the West are financed by private capital. And, in spite of the sensation, widespread to this day, that science is advancing on many fronts, is researching everything it is possible to research and will one day solve each and every one of humanity's problems, to what extent is this actually true? The big pharmaceutical multinationals are far less interested, in terms of keeping their shareholders happy, in any of the illnesses ravaging places in Africa or Asia than in the sore throats, sagging jowls or clogged pores of the

First World. And, in this case, it matters very little whether the problems have a solution or not; for decades, PR and marketing have been used to hide the lack of solutions to the most frivolous western problems. There is also the fact that governments may take a hand in deciding where subsidies end up. And the scientist has no option but to go on working inside a system that inevitably requires finance.

Science is blind. Science does not advance on all possible fronts, only certain ones, which themselves may be abandoned at any moment if there is a lack of commercial benefit or political will. Science will not solve every problem, only some – and sometimes the simplest ones will remain unsolved. And when science says it knows the truth, it lies.

Throughout *The Structure of Scientific Revolutions*, Kuhn intentionally avoided the subject of truths. This thing we call truth does not exist. Science allows us to access an increasingly precise understanding of what nature is to us. But it is incumbent on us to renounce the idea that scientists are increasingly closer to the truth, because their hypotheses always depend on the context in which they have come about. The certainties are consensuses, ephemeral and by no means autonomous.

The scientific process is not an evolution towards that truth we wish to know. Rather, it is a partial construction on the basis of the little that we do know.

And Paul Feyerabend will take these conclusions further still in *Against Method* (1975). For Feyerabend, scientific method as such does not exist: science follows no particular order, and scientific research has barely ever developed in accordance with anything that could be said to resemble an authentic method. In reality, there is always an abundance of anomalies beyond the prevalent paradigm's capacity to explain, though they will be covered up by an ad hoc hypothesis, which allows for a pause and the signalling of a new direction for the subsequent research. According to the precursor of epistemological anarchism, the Copernican revolution was made possible thanks to Galileo's persuasive powers, his fluid style, the fact he wrote in Italian and not Latin, and his decision to address the general populace rather than the academy. And, true, if it had been left to Copernicus himself, this revolution would have taken far longer to come about, or wouldn't have done so at all. But Galileo availed himself of subterfuge, of rhetoric and propaganda. This was how he succeeded in establishing new forms for the interpretation of nature, based on a more abstract observational language, and even managed to get rid of the perspectives that put the new theory in jeopardy: the old observations of the sky with the naked eye were to be ignored in favour of the blurry phenomena now produced through the telescope. And this, to a greater or lesser degree of sophistication, is what happens with every scientific revolution.

Usually, the demands for consistency imposed by the prevailing paradigms mean the rejection of every new hypothesis that contradicts them. And this always favours the oldest theory, rather than the best one. In Feyerabend's view, the proliferation of conjecture would be beneficial for science. He is unstinting in the idea that theoretical anarchism would be a far greater stimulant for progress than restrictive 'law-and-order science'. And so, to create a genuinely creative science, the rational criterion cannot be the only guide; irrationality must be brought into the fold: 'And Reason, at last, joins all those other abstract monsters such as Obligation, Duty, Morality, Truth and their more concrete predecessors, the Gods, which were once used to intimidate man and restrict his free and happy development.'[1]

Human debility is the only explanation for the persistence of scientific slogans like 'truth', 'objectivity', 'clarity' and 'intellectual honesty'; our deep need for security, our ingenuousness and many other of our baser instincts combine to impoverish the diversity and possibilities offered by history.

In a sense, science more closely resembles art than we might think, because there is in fact no real progress in it, but simply, rather, changes in style. Science's direction is determined by the creative imagination and not the universe of facts that surround us.

But the moment we fail to recognize its fictional nature, science becomes just one more ideology. And then it moves away from art and closer to the realm of myth. In spite of the fact that modern science is nothing more than another of the many forms of thought developed by human beings, its many achievements have brought with them an egocentric, self-complacent, uncultured and self-regarding slant, as it demands for itself an absolutely privileged status, with accompanying reverence and submission. As we have seen, it was founded on its own scientific myths and the demand for faith in that which we could not see with our own eyes, and in the current day that makes it the most powerful dogma on the planet.

Thomas S. Kuhn died of lung cancer. Paul Feyerabend, as a consequence of a brain tumour. Both died before their time and due to causes that could have been avoided had science found effective treatments by that time.

It might be thought that if science had saved their lives

---

[1] Paul Feyerabend, *Against Method*. London: Verso, 1988.

– if it had been capable of keeping their consciousnesses animate, these thinking subjects – maybe they would ultimately have come round to the idea of progress.

And yet, neither Kuhn nor Feyerabend ever denied the *utility* of scientific procedure. They always admitted its partial advances and, as far as it was possible for them, tried to encourage them.

What they rejected was the unequivocal status enjoyed by science, its image of progress as an unwavering line towards some kind of truth revealed by the fact of the universe.

The idea of truth is increasingly empty of meaning.

In its place, we ought to speak of fiction and plausibility.

THE PRESENT, HYPERREALITY AND POST-TRUTH

What does being a person consist of in the present day?

Think of someone living in a rural place who gets up with the sun every morning, has no modern technology, no social contact aside from the occasional encounter with someone else working the fields, eats healthily – 'real food' – and who spends all their time from morning till night tending to their plot. Will this person be more or less happy than us? Will they be closer to or further away from whatever it is we are supposed to be?

A primitive man, one of these men who according to Lévi-Strauss had the same structures of rational thought as we do and who could just as well be like you or me if he had been born in this era – was he more faithful than we are to our shared nature? There is the fact that, in living by the sweat of his brow, he was less alienated from the means of production. But there is also the fact that his life was far shorter – and that, throughout, there would have been discomfort, pain and extreme danger all around.

And now, ask yourself this question: is it not also perhaps our nature to behave like fictional beings?

There is no doubt that modern-day society offers us more opportunities than ever before to realize ourselves fully through free and creative activity, which is one of the few things – if not the only one – that can confer meaning on the lives of women and men. At the same time, however, we could be forgiven for wondering: is this vast array of fictions always good for us? And I am not alluding here to their ethical dimension, or questioning whether they are lies that have been fashioned with good or bad intentions; this entire book has been an attempt to discuss lies in a *nonmoral* sense. If we limit ourselves to the problems set in train by their sheer quantity, could we consider the possibility that all of this has got out of hand?

A day in the life of a postmodern person

The postmodern person, just like the modern, mediaeval, ancient or prehistoric person, has barely to wake in the morning before being drawn into the series of lies they are telling the people around them. From the second she drinks her cup of coffee, she is, as ever, obliged to adulate the group that provides her with shelter and security, as a simple matter of survival. Almost without realizing it, she will deploy falsehoods and half-truths in order to protect her loved ones from all that she really feels, and, since this is rather complicated, she will also need to protect herself with a certain amount of self-deception. She will also have no option but to hide her visceral dislike of all those around her who get on her nerves. And, just as in former times, she will need to put on different faces, modulate her tone and present different personalities depending on whether she is interacting with her partner, members of her family, neighbours, acquaintances, friends, work colleagues, rivals, her boss or those who are her enemies.

The difference now being that, from the moment she opens her eyes in the darkness of her bedroom, the postmodern person will find, just there on her bedside table, a glowing window into the new world. Meaning she will need to begin lying before she even gets up and has a stretch.

The postmodern person knows – because this is what she has been trained for – that the different social networks bring with them their own codes of conduct and that she must act differently depending on where she finds herself, even though she might be having interactions in a variety of those places at once. This is something she has got used to over the years. It sometimes seems like it could even be there in her genes. When the postmodern person finds herself on a network that overlaps with her world of work, she will try to hide certain aspects of her life, and act, and even express herself, in a very different way from how she would in confidence. If the platform in question is purely professional, this simulation will go up a notch and she will lie about her capabilities, her experience and all those things that could be in her favour, to the point where she will come to believe that her exaggerated statements correspond with her real past – are a genuine component of her curriculum vitae. When the context is a friendlier one, but not fully intimate, she will still keep her guard somewhat raised and try to present an image of herself that is as close as possible to the person she would like to be. In these moments, the postmodern person will feel an almost complete sense of fulfilment, because, through various digital means, her mental mechanisms of self-deceit are at long last being reinforced. With other people there as an audience, she will make as much of a show as possible of her overblown view of herself, with recourse to everything from photos, videos, filters, lines of poetry, aphorisms, thoughts of her own and thoughts she's stolen from others – and this even when a part of her is aware of the lie, and even when she knows that a part of other people won't ultimately believe it. It makes no difference to her. She will accept the constant challenge presented by social networks to her capacity for untruth; it will make her feel like she's really, intensely alive.

But not everybody has it in them to keep so many different lies, or levels of lying, going at the same time. And the postmodern person is still, after all, a real, embodied creature. Anyone can have a bad day, especially when they still haven't managed to get a decent cup of coffee inside them.

One of these mornings, the postmodern person will grab her mobile phone and, eyes not yet completely open, tap at the screen: 'How cute! Adorable! Want! Congrats! Enjoy!' This will be followed by a long series of smiley faces, dog-emojis and hearts, all of which she will then post in a thread below a photo of somebody's pet that just died of leukaemia.

Then she'll realize what she's done. She'll scramble to delete the comment. But something in this particular app means she won't be able to, she can't get her fingers to obey, and people will already have begun responding to and sharing her faux pas. Her blood will begin to boil; she'll see red. She will try to log on to Twitter, where she has a fake account that she uses to let off steam, although she might accidentally hit the Instagram icon instead. This is usually a place where she lets herself be carried along by the general wave of love and happiness, does her best to increase her friend count and generally reconcile herself with humanity. However, not realizing her error, as soon as she sees a mane of long blonde hair tumbling down somebody's bare back, she will write: 'Stop being such a prick tease, you slut. If what you really want to do is show your boobs, just get it over with. Enough of the innuendo.'

This clearly isn't her day. Plus, something just came to her, though vaguely: that wasn't the woman she was thinking of. She goes and clicks on the woman's profile picture, and recognizes the selfie (in bed, but with perfect make-up) of the girl she has spent the past several months wooing, trotting out all her sweetest lies to that end, and with whom she was on the verge of making a date in a city halfway between where they each live.

Postmodern person closes her eyes and takes a deep breath. She's still got a long day ahead. Initiating sessions; using various profiles on the intranet at work, in the cloud where she shares files, on all the instant messaging groups; checking and replying to messages in her numerous email accounts; maybe surfing anonymously in search of something titillating, or logging into one of her other fake accounts to troll someone or hurt them in some way, leaving comments below the line; allowing her physical location to be tracked as she goes, and at the end of the day being sure to update the platforms she frequents the most. But before any of that, she will get up, go and splash her face and check, on the same touchscreen device, whether the coffee she ordered the previous day has arrived.

All the complexity accumulated on the surface of the world up until the twentieth century, in which the image has taken on greater and greater importance, is now amplified by this digital dimension, which refracts our image of ourselves and projects it with all the intensity of a company brand. But not everyone is equally enthusiastic about this level of self-exposure, or necessarily prepared to curate their image of themselves as though it were a brand. Some will find it difficult to comprehend the multifaceted world unfolding before our eyes, or even to get as far as comprehending the self-image they have almost unintentionally created and with which they fail to identify fully.

The two poles of lying exist simultaneously in the virtual world. On the one hand, there are the anonymous spaces in which we may simply drop all social pretence, with the single lie of a false identity rushing in to replace it – an identity that then gets incorporated into our new and complex dissociated image. And, on the other, there is the registering of your every movement, which adds a new layer to the mask of your habitual identity that is both disproportionate and difficult to control. The experts tell us that people increasingly modify their behaviour when connected to networks that identify who they are. People who listen to music on platforms with a sharing option may stop listening to the things they want to and begin prioritizing instead the image of themselves – or of the part of themselves that comprises their musical tastes – that they wish to project. And the same thing happens on all other online communities. At the same time, the constant demand to make a show of happiness can be difficult to bear. Not purely because of the effort required to demonstrate this permanent state of supposed felicity, but because, as Montesquieu would declare 300 years ago, it isn't really happiness that one aspires to, but being happier than other people. And we always think other people are happier than they are. And, meanwhile, all the data suggests that using social networks on a daily basis triples the risk of depression. Research tells us that being immersed in the digital sphere makes for lower self-esteem, increased feelings of loneliness, and difficulty in developing traditional social skills. And while the distance between my virtual self-projection and my life in the outside world grows ever wider, the impact of the former on the latter increases. Dismissal from a job can even be justified by one's internet use, as a misjudgement when it comes to projecting the image of yourself could get you sacked: not having moved quickly enough to hide an inappropriate photo; a joke that either is in poor taste or could be misunderstood out of context; a criticism of the company you work for or someone higher up in the chain of command who is watching from the shadows; revealing confidential information; or even having neglected to hide your bad spelling. And it is growing increasingly common for couples to break up because of things that happen online or in instant messaging apps. Not only because these can be sources for deception and infidelity, but also because they give us an inflated sense of the opportunities for new relationships, make us succumb to the illusion of comparing our personal happiness with that of others, or possibly because your expectations about your partner – whom you met online – were exaggerated. Recent rumours suggest that Facebook alone was responsible for 28 million break-ups in the space of less than a decade.

Nonetheless, rumours are only rumours.

A real investigation

This story about Facebook would go more or less as follows: on 10 February 2010, the American Academy of Matrimony put a note on its website; this was the first solid reference I managed to find on the subject. It went like this: 'A staggering 81% of leading divorce attorneys say they have seen an increase in the number of cases using social networking evidence in the five years prior.' Shortly afterwards, on 28 February, the magazine *PC World* put its own spin on things: 'The perfect Valentine's tale: if you are separated, or in the process of getting a divorce, keep away from Facebook. According to a recent survey of divorce lawyers in the U.S., Facebook is the "unsurpassed leader" in online evidence of matrimonial infidelity.' And from there the idea gained unstoppable traction. Not because it was good, well-supported journalism, or had the backup of significant specialists, or included relevant data. But, rather, because it was the kind of news piece the media are desperate for, because they know it sells, though they all know it's just more eyewash for their readers. CNN picked up on the story, Reuters went out with it too, and it began popping up everywhere. In Spain, *La Razón* went with the headline 'Your Facebook Posts Can Be Used against You in Court', while *El Mundo* said 'Facebook Responsible for 20% of Divorces'. The idea progressively morphed. On 3 February 2011, *Marketing Directo* declared that 'thanks to Facebook, we can now find out our friends' marital status . . . There are at least 15 million newly single individuals on this social network.' A fortnight later, in the Colombian daily *El Espectador*, this translated into the headline: 'Facebook Responsible for 28 Million Separations'. This particular article, in an attempt at credibility, as well as ambiguously quoting law firms in the US, made the first mention of *Cyberpsychology, Behavior, and Social Networking*, though without providing the date, issue number or author of the piece cited. But in a publication specializing in studying the social and psychological impact of social networks, it is easy to find data on this subject. I was quite disoriented by the profusion of references, and it wasn't until a few days before I came to write this that I managed to track down the statistics offered up by *El Espectador*. They were in an article entitled 'Cheating, Breakup, and Divorce: Is Facebook Use to Blame?'.[1] However, I was unable to find any mention of the eye-catching figure of 28 million. The trail went cold; I began to lose hope. I found out that this magazine had changed title in 2011 to *CyberPsychology & Behavior*. Again, I thought there might be some hope. But I still couldn't find anything to corroborate the number. And that was when I gave up on that aspect of my investigation. Soon WhatsApp would come to be mentioned far more frequently than Facebook, while the same 28 million break-ups would continue to be cited. And then this entirely unfounded notion went viral: everyone from *Europa Press* to the Spanish radio station *Cadena Ser*, the newspapers *La Vanguardia* and *ABC*, *La Razón* and *El Mundo* each repeating the story (this time replacing Facebook with WhatsApp), along with *Las Provincias*, *La Gaceta*, *El Correo*, the Mexican *Televisa* and *Excélsior*, the Venezuelan *Semana*, *El País* in Colombia, *CN23* in Argentina, Telemadrid, Antena 3, Andreu Buenafuente's programme on Spanish TV channel La Sexta, and the show co-hosted by Julia Otero and Carlos Herrera on Spanish radio station Onda Cero . . . Eventually, on 11 October 2013, the online paper *Eldiario.es* put a stop to the epidemic:

> Over the last week, you will have read or heard on Spanish-speaking news networks that WhatsApp has not only revolutionized the way we communicate, but that it is also responsible for the breakup of 28 million couples across the world. This has been one of the most read and shared pieces on the Internet. Google News shows us over 130 references on different Spanish media outlets. In Spain it has been cited in print and online. It has also been aired on radio and TV. But it is a lie.

[1] *Cyberpsychology, Behavior, and Social Networking* 16.10 (2013), pp. 717–20.

I'm grateful to Ignasi Roviró, at the Universidad Ramon Llull, for having put me on the right track with his article 'WhatsApp vs Couples', in *Revista d'Etnologia de Catalunya* 41 (2016), pp. 37–46.

Rumours are only rumours, and on the new technologies of the Internet they have found the perfect medium to self-propagate. And journalists, who are supposed to be precisely the ones who contain them, seem to have added their number to the same vertiginous tendency – the new, non-source-checking, copy-and-paste journalism, overwhelmed as it is by the quantity and velocity of the news, each inversely proportional to the available resources: in a world flooded by free information, the press is going through the worst crisis in its history, unable to find new ways of financing itself. The polity meanwhile are not prepared to pay for information when they can get it – even if of lesser quality – for free.

Nobody seems to notice what little good it does to be able to access all the news at the click of a button, if it comes accompanied by every contradictory piece of news. Like in some library of Babel, in our digitalized reality there is a counter-theory for every theory. In our present-day world, for every registered fact, every piece of data, all theories and hypotheses, there are replicas that say the exact opposite. For every argument, a counter-argument. It makes no difference if it is a discussion of politics or a list of suggestions for good health. It makes no difference if we are talking about economic issues, a detailed explanation of the origins of some armed conflict or how to look after your baby. Every reality has at least two different versions, and that which is good today will be bad tomorrow – only to turn out to be good again some time afterwards. We live in a moment when search engines are capable of dragging everything up, which is why the information era is also the disinformation era.

With the globalization of markets, societies and cultures, we have seen the arrival of the greatest plurality of perspectives imaginable – and, almost at the same time, their inevitable homogenization. And in such a context, neither the dominant economic nor political interests – accustomed to dominating the media ever since their inception – have the slightest intention of failing to use the Internet to spread the ideology that supports them. One need only glance at the Net to see that capitalism remains the real motor of contemporary aesthetics, not only because advertising invades everything, but because most of the brands and trends end up working in line with market interests. Political parties also use everything the new technologies put at their disposal in their bids to outdo their opponents, and certain governments – like those in Russia, North Macedonia and Romania – have even been accused of creating websites containing fake news, and armies of bots to disseminate them, as a way of engineering elections, pumping up or overthrowing foreign leaders, altering the behaviour or beliefs of voters and, ultimately, weakening their rival powers.

In this atmosphere of confusion, information overload and superabundant images – of digital manipulation, fake news, fake profiles and great swarms of bots – in which different levels of reality exist alongside one another and social networks are endlessly multiplying, we see the arrival of the new – and itself misleading – term 'post-truth'.

The invention of post-truth, in a time when new inventions are needed on an almost daily basis to feed the information machine, is therefore another consequence of the overwhelming sensation that grips us – the feeling that we are at a kind of peak in our capacity for creating and keeping up all our fictions. But this is at the same time another lie, or, if one prefers, a meta-lie, because it fails to tell the truth about the newness of the kind of deceit currently occurring. Or have politicians in fact not lied from the moment someone stood for election? Have they not always availed themselves of populism, rhetoric, empty arguments, false promises, the vilification of opponents? Are sophism, sleights of hand, falsification and propaganda not in fact old hat?

Vlad the Impaler and post-truth: the origin

When Vlad the Impaler became ruler of Wallachia in 1456, he had already spent many years leading the fight against the Turks, seeking allies and learning military tactics. And it would not be long before his cruel reputation spread the length and breadth of Europe. Implacable as a ruler and strategist, this led him to become virtually the only obstacle to the eastward expansion of the Ottoman Empire. However, what the prince couldn't have foreseen was the invention of printing, nor the way it would immediately be put to work in defamation campaigns.

During his reign, Vlad the Impaler put curbs on the privileges of the nobility, was unforgiving to the cities that failed to fall in line and won himself an enormous array of opponents. And so, satirical posters soon began to appear that sought to put a dent in his image, both detailing and overplaying his atrocities. In Transylvania, on the streets of places such as Brașov and Sibiu, with their large numbers of German and Saxon settlers unwilling to pay him tribute, thousands of libellous pamphlets were distributed. And all across the neighbouring regions, this same material, printed in Germanic cities like Nuremberg, Lübeck, Leipzig and Strasbourg, began to appear. All discussed Vlad's skirmishes, dressing them up with the bloodiest, most ludicrous details. Etched wooden reliefs even began to appear for the benefit of the illiterate.

Like any lie worth its salt, those slanderous stories had an element of truth. But while Vlad the Impaler was out applying his personal idea of strength and justice, something completely unprecedented was being hatched against him: perhaps the first ever international campaign to blacken a person's name. A manoeuvre that would soon involve not only Transylvanians and Germans, but also Polish, Lithuanians, Russians, Hungarians, Rumelians and Ottomans. A ground-breaking and barefaced attempt to use fiction to overturn reality.

Vlad found enemies around him on all sides, and it wasn't long before his only backer, his brother-in-law Matthias Corvinus, King of Hungary, also fell into the manipulative mesh. At a time when their alliance appeared unbreakable, Corvinus was presented with three letters – supposedly intercepted, supposedly from Vlad to Mehmed II, Mahmud Pasha and Stefan of Moldavia, containing offers to join forces with the sultan to defeat the Hungarians. In later centuries, these would be proven forgeries, but at the time the king flew into a rage and had his brother-in-law thrown in the dungeons, where he stayed for fourteen long years. It proved to be the beginning of the end.

Matthias Corvinus the Wise decided to take the lead in the international campaign, which would continue throughout the following decade, and the next, and for many decades after Vlad's death on the battlefield in 1476.

The German minstrel Michael Beheim, one of Corvinus's retainers, wrote a poem called *The History of a Despot Named Dracula, Prince of Wallachia*, describing an episode in which he had two monks impaled in order that their souls would go to heaven, and how for good measure he then had their donkey impaled when it began to bray at its masters' demise. Following Corvinus's proposal, Gabriele Rangoni, Bishop of Eger, wrote about the rumour that Vlad, while incarcerated, captured rats which he would cut up into small pieces and impale on sticks; he was, in other words, inveterately evil. Corvinus's court historian, Antonio Bonfini, filled his *Historia Pannonica* (1495) to bursting with anecdotes of Vlad's rare cruelty, including one in which some Turkish emissaries, refusing to take off their turbans, had them nailed to their heads. These histories continued to be told by the Slavic and Russian peoples throughout the sixteenth and seventeenth centuries, with Vlad consistently described as a demented psychopath, sadist and appalling murderer. And similar was written by the Germans – except that, with the arrival of the printing press, these became the first bestsellers in Europe. In fact, the editions published in Nuremberg (1499) and in Strasbourg (1500), in an attempt to improve sales, had woodcut prints on the covers showing Vlad dining amidst the impaled corpses of his victims.

Of course, none of these chroniclers, so far away in time and space from the events, had any way of checking the shocking details.

The legend surrounding the Prince of Wallachia was always constructed at a distance. The nickname 'the Impaler' – now such a specific association – was in fact never assigned to him in life, but only posthumously in 1550.

The theorists of post-truth, and certain political analysts, point to one of its essential elements being its supposedly novel appeal to people's emotions with the objective of altering public opinion. But did the propaganda directed against Vlad the Impaler not feed on emotion, on atavistic fear, on human weakness? And was it not conceived precisely to manipulate people's beliefs? How is that campaign, begun in the fifteenth century, different from contemporary post-truth? They also argue that post-truth relegates the opinions of experts to the background, and even the facts themselves; it constitutes a truth above and beyond fact – part of a post-factual politics. And is this not exactly what has always defined lying in general, and political lying in particular? Didn't the Sophists of the fifth century BC – all of whom wished to take up public positions – show that the function of rhetoric was to convince, and not to bring us closer to the truth? And in the fourth century BC, didn't the Socratic Cynics try to dismantle the dominant ideas and most respected philosophers using irony or satire? Hasn't every single totalitarian regime sought to rewrite the facts, recruiting officially sanctioned spokespersons and discrediting any experts expressing contrary opinions? And after the printing press appeared, were these prescriptions not also met by the pamphlet wars, like Luther's against the Catholic Church, or the endless Elizabethan pamphlet wars, or the controversies throughout the English Civil War and the American Revolution in which pamphleteering played a part? So what is left that is truly original within this concept of post-truth? We might suppose that what really sets it apart is its disinformational aspect, but, 2,500 years ago, Sun Tzu was already talking about how to create discord among one's enemies by generating false information and using spies to spread it. We could perhaps venture that the key is in digital manipulation, but we know that the airbrushing of photographs and creation of photomontages is as old as photography itself, and counterfeiting something absolutely integral to human beings. Clearly, post-truth is only the most recent link in our long chain of fictions. There is nothing qualitative that would allow us to speak of such a thing as post-truth; the only distinctive thing about the present moment is quantity: the new technologies have combined with globalization to increase the reverberation of such untruths exponentially; deceitful manoeuvres have a wider reach and greater consequences than ever before, but at the same time the average person is far more aware of the huge farce unfolding around them.

Technological democratization has allowed everyone to have a say. And this brings us to the genuinely novel aspect of the times in which we live. Though economic and political power remain in the same hands – those of the select few who still conserve the true capacity to spread information – everybody can now express an opinion. And everybody does opine, of course, on all subjects – especially about all subjects. The important thing is to have an opinion and to speak it loudly.

The time we are living in, therefore, is the opinion era. And our overwhelming need to give an opinion on everything brings into being a forest so densely woven, so impenetrable, that everybody is able to shout and nobody can hear. This, in practice, means we've all gone back to losing our voices. When everybody is a writer; when everybody speaks for the sake of it; when the least informed person only need click on a few links to be able to publish on a subject; when the majority does nothing but copy information from somewhere else; when just about all that happens on social networks is the sharing, reproduction and propagation of other people's ideas, phrases, images, mistakes or lies – it becomes difficult to find anything of value in the interminable undergrowth.

There is no such thing as post-truth: it is the overgrown chaos of opinion that has taken control of virtual reality, diminishing it, turning it into a rarefied sort of place in which rumours take root, in which it is stunningly easy for hoaxes, made-up articles and chains of fraudulent messages to spread, and mountains of digital trash accumulate, and conspiracy theories and global paranoia intensify.

If we zoom out just a little, postmodernity has indeed had a lot to do with all of this. Over the years, its relativism has succeeded in filtering into society and – though such a vision did play a part in the crisis of certain values that needed to be ousted, and to put things in their rightful place – it also smoothed the way for opinions to begin to dominate. These same opinions – *doxa* – were for Plato the lowest and most deceptive forms of knowledge; the speakers of these *doxa* in the Agora, he said, used false knowledge and suggestion for their personal gain and social betterment, and their words always moved faster than their thoughts. It's like we've gone back in time. As though a journey of so many centuries were about to bring us back to the very beginning. In principle, postmodern deconstructionism ought to provide an intellectual, playful, pleasurable fictional aspect among so much impenetrability and devastation. And that has happened, because it has found in the Internet the ideal medium to go on branching out: intertextuality has been given a boost by hyperlinks and new multimedia formats; artistic mock-ups, pastiche, gameplaying, interactivity, performances, all these things have acquired a dimension of which they could never previously have dreamed; and there has been a proliferation of works – novels, essays, films, TV series – which take as their very themes falsification, virtual reality, social networks, the world of hackers, simulation and the simulacrum, globalization, media manipulation, international intrigue, political corruption, classified secrets, the lies of multinational corporations and financial speculation. And it would be impossible to put a number on the critical works that, in turn, analyse all these questions, such that readers and spectators, on whom all the complexities of the new forms of contemporary lying come crashing down every day, become even more aware of all the levels of imposture spreading out around them, which again will add new levels of awareness and even more labyrinths in which to get lost. Postmodernity, however, functioned like a Trojan horse. And alongside all these aesthetic elements, a great wave of opinion has also been unleashed, which, like a torrent, has coursed through our shared spaces, occupying every last corner. And, between them, they have all played a part in erecting this jungle-like hyperreality in which we are all caught up, barely able to move.

Baudrillard said that hyperreality is an excess of reality. A substitution for the real. But Baudrillard was wrong. When was reality ever real? Have human beings ever really had contact with reality? If we take as our starting position our incapacity for breaking through to the real in itself, if we accept the premise that reality has always been a construction based on untruths, then hyperreality is nothing more than the same mirage intensified. As with post-truth, it is yet another step in the same direction for the metaphorical animal that we are. Hyperrealism is the sublimation of our perception of the world, the continuation of our unstoppable fictionalizing tendencies.

In the Palaeolithic, clay and fats were used to alter people's appearances; later on, make-up techniques would develop; now, over the cosmetic layers of a model, we also apply digital design, a deception on top of a deception with which we seek to take our idealizing processes still further. This is fiction castling behind fiction – a dangerous loop. Thus, the laws of hyperreality dictate that when a supermodel, who serves as an archetype for normal women, loses weight, it has an immediate influence on those around her, but when normal women start losing weight as a consequence, the supermodel will be obliged to become even thinner still, so that she remains different from everyone else and can at the same time continue serving as a reference point in the society. Constant digital innovations have allowed us to go even further with such idealizations, even though the perversity of this circular process is self-evidently unsustainable. And the most unsettling part is that fashions and hyperreality advance unexpectedly, randomly; the governing norms have been what they are purely because it was possible for them to be so. This is because postmodernity, in as much as it is a manifestation of late capitalism, left us in the hands of the exigencies of capital, which is blind. For the moment, these exigencies have pushed us in the direction of an impoverishment of nuance and texture, in favour of concretion and clarity. But clarity about what? Hyperreality is to reality what present-day high-definition pornography is to sex: more than a sublimation of it, it is a caricature. This is where so many games of make-believe have really brought us.

And social networks are the maximum caricaturization of this hyperreality of appearances, in which we all seek to *appear* to be what others expect us to be.

We live in the opinion era – baseless opinions, opinions with no underpinning in research or analysis, unqualified opinions, opinions that contradict fact, opinions for the sake of having an opinion – and with the idea that all opinions are equal. On the basis of these, relativism has penetrated our virtual hyperreality, in greater measure and in far more mediocre fashion than anything the postmodernists could have imagined.

And this vast, conjecture-contaminated virtuality put the finishing touches – along with the lying in our private lives and social forms of lying that have always been there – to the three levels of lying that converge on the contemporary subject.

That's why it's now so necessary to cut back.

We have to get rid of all the excess, as well as stopping obeying the dictates of the market alone, if we want to avoid dying of asphyxiation.

If we want to avoid dying of fiction.[2]

[2] Notice that this entire chapter is based on one big lie – namely, the ethnocentric fallacy according to which the majority of humanity today belongs to a more or less free, more or less advanced society with the benefit of some level of wellbeing. This overlooks the fact that, of the 7.4 billion or so inhabitants of Earth, only 3.5 billion use the Internet. And, of this last group, only 1 billion belong to developed countries that can guarantee an effective digital inclusiveness, allowing them access to all content, education, security, the power to buy things or the freedom to pursue their goals. That is, for 6 out of every 7 people in the world, the above-described fictional excesses are not part of their reality, and in some cases not even remotely.

LOVE

And then, one day, in the midst of the world's illusion, the artifice of culture and the stage sets of cities rearing up around us, trapped and tangled in all the lies and growing more and more tired of playing the game, finding ourselves on the verge of giving up the search for meaning and simply throwing in the towel – we fall in love.

They meet, him and her, in an absolutely magic and unrepeatable moment, just as they have always dreamed they would. It is immediately apparent to them both that they were made for one another, that it was written in the stars. And, at last, they manage to experience something authentic, and true love emerges. A love that will perhaps last forever.

And of course, once again, it is all a lie.

At no other time in our lives will we be so thoroughly duped as when love takes hold. It is a moment so crucial to the survival of the species that all the sociocultural myths and lies that have always been so confounding to us will find an even more powerful ally – namely, the biochemistry of our own organism, which will betray and captivate us as no other drug in the world can. No psychoactive substance exists that is capable of fooling us for such a long period, while at the same time letting us believe we are being true to ourselves and acting of our own free will.

He has come to the party expecting to meet someone he knows. An interesting discussion has struck up in the past few minutes, and he has gone over with the sense that he might still make some useful contacts. He has been feeling somewhat stressed at work in recent weeks, but he tries not to let it show. And, though he doesn't even know it, the cortisol in his bloodstream – caused by the stress – makes him more open to a relationship that will help him to relax.

He undoes the top button of his shirt and loosens his tie. He takes a deep breath, trying to take the edge off his unease, and looks around. He thinks he's casting around for familiar faces, ones he thinks he's seen down passageways and on the Web, and that might signify the possibility of promotion. He is also aware, vaguely, of having briefly glanced at the women in the main party room. There's no avoiding that, he says to himself. He is also unaware of the true nature of this quick casting around; our species has been programmed to interpret as quickly as possible the largest amount of genetic information about the opposite sex. To the species as a whole, it doesn't matter in the slightest that procreating and having offspring are the last things on his mind this evening; in moments like this, he is subject not only to the imperative to reproduce, but to the crucial importance of finding the most suitable genes possible for the job, and of his potential partner being in the optimal reproductive condition, which is his children's best chance for survival. This means that, when he observed the women in the room, his gaze paused several times on different faces, seeking a symmetry that could confirm an absence of childhood infections or nutritional problems. And, at the same dizzying speed, his gaze darted towards their breasts, which are a sign of fertility. And finally, towards the waists and hips of all the young ladies present;

he was particularly attracted by those whose waists were at least 70 per cent narrower than their hips, which is a clear indication of their ability to conceive and bear children. He is aware of none of this. It wasn't a conscious decision, and he hasn't registered any of it. His brain – which is the true traitor and species enabler – has taken over.

And then he, whose name could be Carlos, or Esteban, sees her.

For her part, she is feeling distracted. It's just another night, and moments ago she was thinking that she may as well have stayed at home, without these unforgiving heels – she could be putting her feet up on the sofa, not having to look perfect or make all this effort to get on with people. But she hasn't really been feeling that great at home either, recently. She is completely unaware of it, but cortisol is also running through her bloodstream and making her feel a lot of anxiety. She isn't enjoying her own company like she used to and has begun to miss the feeling of security she's felt when in relationships. Social pressure also contributes to her recent predisposition to finding a mate. In the eyes of society, she's getting too old to be single still. All her girlfriends who are in relationships assure her that it's better being with someone, not having to go out night after night. And then there's her mother – above all, her mother.

Then she sees him.

Their eyes meet; it is a moment without compare. They feel their hearts begin to pound.

She watches as he comes over, swaying his shoulders almost imperceptibly and swinging his arms, in a way that makes him appear bulkier than he is. And more attractive. His eyebrows are bushy and he has a square chin, signs that he produced large amounts of testosterone in puberty and might have the makings of a good father. Again, none of this occurs to her at a conscious level. With her brain and her entire nervous system going all out to try to deceive her, she thinks about the thrill of his gaze, about how much she loves the song playing in the background, and whether he is really just going to walk up and speak to her.

'My name's Esteban', the man says, offering his hand to shake.

The young lady takes his hand, but rather than shaking it tugs on it to draw them closer, and then kisses him on the cheek, in a show – this time conscious – of warmth and openness.

'Violeta', she whispers. Followed by a laugh.

They hold one another's gaze again, now just half a metre apart.

And each feels quite sure this is their soulmate.

Nonetheless, the myth of the soulmate, or your 'other half', goes all the way back to Aristophanes and is, in reality, a fantastical tale that has only become more potent over time, giving us exaggerated hopes for relationships – and, with them the resultant frustrations, and disillusion.[1] But it

---

[1] In *The Banquet*, Plato attributes the origin of this myth to Aristophanes, who seems to have declared that there were three sexes at the beginning of time: the masculine, which was descended from the Sun; the feminine, descendant of the Earth; and the androgynous, the most imperfect of the three and a descendant of the Moon. These primitive humans had four arms, four legs and two faces. And were all such reckless creatures that they came up with the foolhardy idea of climbing into heaven and taking on the gods. Zeus was enraged, and decided to punish them:

> 'I am not going to destroy them', he said to his listeners on Mount Olympus. 'But, to reduce their impudence, I will split them in half. They will become weaker and have to walk in a straight line, standing on just two legs. And if their impudence is undiminished, I will again split them in half, so that they will have to walk on a single leg.'

is a tale ingrained in their culture, and neither of them can avoid being taken in by it. Although, at this stage, it doesn't actually have that much of an influence. A chemical army has been marching through each of them for a little while now, rendering them incapable of changing tack. Their mesencephalic nucleuses have begun pumping out large quantities of dopamine and norepinephrine, which are responsible for euphoria, excitement and desire, while their serotonin levels have dropped dramatically. This is how the amygdala, which has spent millions of years accumulating knowledge, manages to inhibit the areas of the brain where negative emotions and critical judgement are processed. The way this young pair explain it to themselves, though, is by recourse to mythology – Roman mythology, on this occasion, which turned Eros into Cupid and armed him with bow and arrows. They simply think they must be lovestruck.

'From over there, your eyes were the only thing I could see', says Esteban. Not true.

He does gaze into them now. At the same time, however, his brain is carefully examining the distance between her eyes, the distance between her eyes and nose, and checking that the width of her nose is in proportion with that of her mouth. In every case following a golden ratio that certifies the presence of healthy, strong genes. Large

From the moment of this splitting, the two human halves would go to enormous lengths to find one another, and, when they succeeded, never wished to be separated again. For Aristophanes, of the three resultant kinds of love, that which occurs between a man and a woman is the lowest, in that it consists of the androgynous union of two opposites; the love between two women is a level higher; while the love between two men is without doubt the most noble, and therefore superior.

And this is the foundation of the myth of the soulmate.

eyes are important, yes. But sparse eyebrows and a small, pointed chin are as well, denoting as they do that Violeta produced large amounts of progesterone and oestrogen in puberty, which will mean she has efficient reproductive apparatus.

She, a person who would normally have shown her disdain for such cheesy nonsense with an ironic comeback, is enchanted. Again, she smiles, clapping her hands either side of her face in a gesture of false modesty.

The dopamines excite them and make them attentive to all the new stimuli. And the norepinephrine means they will still be able to remember the tiniest details of this moment for months to come. This greeting is enough to enable Violeta to call Esteban's smell to mind.

'What cologne is that?' she asks, but this in reality is a way of getting to breathe in the smell given off by the skin on his neck.

And though she doesn't even realize it, as chance would have it – here is the magic part, here is fate – she is ovulating. Her organism is especially predisposed to procreating. And in this particular moment the smell of androsterone, which she would usually find unpleasant – with its connotations of being at the gym or in a truck drivers' bar – is captivating to her.

'I love it', she says in his ear.

As does her primitive brain: the histocompatibility of his body odour tells her that they have complementary immune systems, and have no shared familial ties among their ancestors, which will make for far more resistant children.

Luckily for her, the fact she's ovulating has added effects: her skin is brighter; there is an added sharpness to her voice, which makes it more attractive, because instinctually he will interpret this as a sign of higher oestrogen; and, most importantly of all, her own smell has changed and she will be bursting with copulins, which will make her irresistible to just about any man in the vicinity.

Esteban is spellbound. He has never felt anything like this, he thinks. The drop in serotonin means, in these opening moments, that he has eyes only for her. The first signs of an obsession begin to manifest. She seems the most attractive woman in the world. It is beyond him to imagine he is being duped, and that the copulin now in his lungs has completely nullified his cognitive capacity to evaluate Violeta's true attractiveness. In fact, if it weren't for this biochemical mirage, he would find her fairly ordinary-looking.

But he feels electrified, and starts talking. Nonstop. He wants to tell her everything about himself.

She listens with interest. If she is to become pregnant by him, it means a much longer-term commitment on her side, and her feminine instinct – unlike that of the male – needs more than just the genetic information she has managed to discern through visual and olfactory observation. And, though they do help, his tasteful silk tie, stylish shoes and the dapper haircut which makes him so cute aren't enough. Her primitive brain needs more information, actual facts to prove he can be trusted, is a man of means, both in a position to enter into a relationship and able to offer her security. This is why, between laughter, convinced that she is being open and sincere, even deferential, Violeta peppers him with questions.

Later in the evening, they will make love.

And, under the effects of the hormones and the neurotransmitters, it will indeed be a unique experience. The dopamine will have flooded their brains' pleasure centres, in the same way cocaine does, and their senses will be open to the slightest stimulation. So much as brushing skin will be hugely pleasurable. She will have a chance to establish the testosterone levels in his saliva. He will get to satiate himself again on more copulins, this time in her vaginal fluids. The visual stimuli, seeing one another naked for the first time, will seem to them charged with significance. The music she plays on her mobile phone will penetrate their senses with unusual intensity, and they will remember each and every melody for weeks or months to come. The same goes for the smells in the bedroom, the texture of the sheets, the way in which the light breaks through the window at dawn. Everything will be etched in their memories. Even if these heightened perceptions won't be matched by an accompanying lucidity. Quite the opposite, which is what makes up the deceit. Both their critical faculties and their normal states of awareness will have been completely sidelined in the process.

New changes will come over Esteban and Violeta in the days that follow.

The reward system unleashed in their pleasure centres will give rise to a strong addiction. Both of them will want more of the same, and both will be unable to avoid going back for another hit. They will yearn to see, smell and touch each other again. And they will think of nothing but sex with one another, about doing it as many times as they can. Nature needs to be sure that their mating has had the desired effect. To which end, it will continue manipulating the minds of its victims: they will feel emotionally and physically dependent; they will start to act compulsively, obsessively, able to think of nothing but each other; and they will have mood swings more associated with teenagers or drug addicts. They will also temporarily transform their personalities to please the other. And they will distort reality as they never have before, and never will again – at least, unless they find themselves falling in love once more.

'I can't live without you.'

Over the following months, Esteban and Violeta will continually remind one another of the details of the night they met. The song that was playing in that first moment, their first look, the first kiss. They will adapt and perfect the story so that it's easier to evoke, turning it into the founding memory of their relationship, the first of many. Chemistry will have wrought such havoc on them that any unforeseen obstacle to the relationship will only end up strengthening it. In adversity, the so-called 'Romeo and Juliet' effect will only intensify their bond.

To the extent that everything is pre-written in our biology, however, we can't say that either of them has had a choice in any part of the process.

And, long before a year is out, everything will have changed again. On one hand, the usual cultural inventions will contribute to the consolidation of their relationship. Because of the myth of monogamy, the lovers will be made to believe that this is the only possible form a relationship can take, accepting the lie that it is the most natural thing and has been present in every age and culture, rather than being a formula installed principally by the Christian church in the Middle Ages and spread across Europe through its colonial system. There is the marriage myth as well, which will lead them to think this is the only sensible direction for their passion to take – for all that in ancient Greece there wasn't even a word to designate 'marriage', while in ancient Rome chastity was not considered a virtue. And a large number of sociocultural myths besides – such as fidelity, jealousy or a belief in free will – will put the finishing touches to the deceit. And yet, at the same time, our own physiology will have a second, far more efficient strategy in reserve. Following on from the initial barrage of neurotransmitters, a longer-term offensive will now take place, with hormones taking the lead: he will be flooded with vasopressin and she with oxytocin, making them feel as though they have merged into a single thing. The madness of passion will give way to a calmer, if bewildered, happiness.

There was nothing Esteban was looking for that night. Nor Violeta, in spite of all the pressure she was under. When precisely did that change? Was there a moment when we can really say they had the power to decide? Or were there deeper forces at work?

And, nonetheless, once they have lived together for a number of years, they will have accumulated many shared experiences, and the caudate nucleuses in their brains will have created a detailed store of these. Intimate, reciprocal confessions; bringing about good and bad moments for one another. They will have not only shared memories now, but also habits, likings, and places and friends in common. Plus, eventually, children. With every passing day, the inconveniences that would come with breaking up will start to outweigh anything on the other side of the scales: the children will bring new social compromises, economic dependence, a fear of change, a fear of starting again, fear of being alone, fear of getting old. And if either of them ever considered getting out of the relationship, it will become increasingly difficult. That will never, in fact, have been an easy option.

And yet, even though chance, the suitability of the circumstances and nature all conspired against the freedom of Esteban and Violeta, the species has further complications planned for the two of them.

In its immemorial search for the best genes and for survival, the species has learned that a certain amount of infidelity will be to its benefit, increasing genetic diversity and the probabilities of success. This means that not only men are programmed for it. Women will also feel the impulse for extramarital sexual relations, even if it is only when they are ovulating that their biology will give them the necessary push. Everything will always be calculated in terms of investment.

And neither will the chemistry of monogamy and enduring love last forever. In spite of the persistent myth of eternal passion, the dopamines and the norepinephrine won't go on being produced for long. And neither will the levels of vasopressin and oxytocin stay stable forever. After two to six years, the organism will be incapable of continuing to generate these biochemical reactions when the same person is seen or touched, even if that person's name is Esteban or Violeta.

There will be very few exceptions to the reduction of hormones and neurotransmitters in our nervous and endocrine systems. Only certain couples – those who are particularly active and creative when it comes to reinventing themselves – will be able to feel these emotions over again.

And when, as in the majority of cases, the break-up comes, when not only feelings but even memories themselves suddenly change, when everything they have experienced is cast in a different light, and – just like that – their love gives way to hate, there will finally be the undeniable impression of having been under a spell all along.

DEATH

In the final phase of our life there awaits a sensation very similar to the one we have experienced in the aftermath of break-ups: the sensation of existential illusions being shattered.

Of waking from a dream.

It is only at the end of our days that, in moments of lucidity spurred by the imminence of death, the full implications of everything being a lie become clear to us.

The individual who has allowed the years to drift by, immersed in the lethargy of various routines and meekly obeying all the specious constructs of culture – the social, political and economic lies – can feel only one thing in old age: the disquiet that comes with possibly having wasted one's life. Anyone who has failed to rebel against the prevailing lies, and never made an attempt to bring their own fictions to bear, will inevitably feel something along the same lines. That they never did what they wanted. That they ended up living a life they did not want to live. That they ought to have comprehended this far sooner, and broken through all the deceptive norms, and renounced the whole charade. And those who have furthermore lived trapped beneath the entelechy of capitalism, or any other form of economic control, will also add to these: the sensation of having spent their lives working for other people, of the fruits of their labours having been carried off by someone else and that now, with everything wrung out of them, they are going to quit the world just the same as – or worse off than – when they first landed on it.

And after the dream, what is there?

What will my death mean? We know that after we die nothing awaits us, nothing that has anything to do with my self or my awareness. But, once the fallacy of the soul's immortality has been refuted, what impact will my death have on this illusory world? From what we can observe in life, none whatsoever. Nothingness, once again.

Only those I am closest to will really be affected by my death. One or two people – five, perhaps. A few dozen more will feel the loss of me for a number of days, shed a tear, spend some minutes thinking of me with a certain intensity, though apart from that they will carry on as normal. As though it couldn't be otherwise. Only a handful of people will come to my funeral, and for some of them it will be an inconvenience – one more obligation in this world of pure appearance. Most of the people who know me, if they hear of my death, will do nothing more than express condolences in a tweet, a line lost among thousands, a matter of a few seconds' thought. If I were someone famous, maybe it would be thousands of tweets and their accompanying retweets, circulating widely online for a few brief days. And after that, nothing. The world will follow its course unchanged. Nobody's death makes any difference.

Nobody's death stops other people from eating, sleeping, laughing or going on living their own delusions.

Almost none of us have any idea about the bulk of our grandparents' lives, who they were and what they really felt. Even more so the lives of our great-grandparents. Just as our grandchildren will have no idea about us, and our great-grandchildren will forget us entirely.

The individual is of no importance. All that matters is the species.

The only consolation – a partial one – lies in the fact that, once we have understood that identity is an imposture, that we live our lives clinging to illusions, manipulated in every single sphere by deceptions within and without, and that the only remaining thing is the vanishingly small point of awareness bounded deep inside us, this loss isn't such a great tragedy either.

Who could possibly bemoan the loss of this self, so barely perceptible, nestled in some corner of my brain matter? Have I not placed too much value on this tiny thing that repeatedly causes me to wake up inside my body? This detail aside, once free of the mask of identity, I am almost exactly the same as everybody else. I am other people.

The individual does not matter. It's everybody else that does.

SO, WHAT IS THERE?

But if all is lies, if our brain even deceives us in leading us to believe that our representation of reality is reality itself, what is there behind this whole illusion? What remains when we take away each and every one of the lies we have discussed over the course of this book?

The irreducible self remains. Descartes's old thinking subject.

In a certain sense, the Cartesian 'cogito' is now even more reduced. Not so much because we have stripped back its identity, as due to the fact we aren't even sure whether it is this self that makes all the decisions, or the unconscious in its stead. On top of which, in terms of brain signals, we now know that decisions actually occur as many as 7 seconds before we become consciously aware of them.

In any case, in some way or another, and whether we understand it or not, there remains a subject that thinks, that imitates, that comes up with metaphors, that lies, that deceives and is deceived.

There have been many serious attempts to reconstruct this minimal unit of the thinking subject – Kant's *Critique of Pure Reason* (1781) being one. However, faced with the impossibility of demonstrating the existence of the thing-in-itself or numen, all the pure concepts of understanding or Kantian categories – along with his a priori conditions for sensory experience – have ended up falling on this side of the subject. Even those conditions – space and time – will only in the end be as they are for *me*, a mark of *my* sensory experience, but we know nothing of them beyond the confines of our own minds. Again, we see the same thing happen, though with far more deliberation, in Schopenhauer's work – to mention just a couple of notable examples. In *The World as Will and Representation* (1819), with Kantian proposals as his departure point, he maintains on the one hand the existence of the subject of representation and, on the other, that of the object, structured by the a priori apparatuses of time, space and causality. But nothing about this object – none of the natural creations, organic or inorganic, that populate it – have a real existence beyond the representation, similar to what we see with the veil of maya in the Vedanta, or Calderón de la Barca's dream.

These attempts to enlarge the thinking subject by philosophers such as Kant and Schopenhauer give us a great deal of insight into the way we are in the world, and the way we project the world. But here we are still, trapped inside.

There are times when we can still feel our situation to be the one described by the philosopher and sci-fi writer Olaf Stapledon, summarized by Borges in the following way:

> The universe consists of a single person – or rather, of a single consciousness – and of the mental processes that pertain to this consciousness. This person (who is naturally you, the reader) has been created in this same moment, complete with a full array of autobiographical, familial, historical, topographical, astronomical and geological

memories, among which figures, let us say, the unreal situation of beginning to read these lines.[1]

So, is there nothing else besides?

Possibly; possibly not. But what is certain is that, finding ourselves in this place, as I said much earlier on in this book, we have no option but to lie, to speculate and to launch into the hypothesis of the world's existence.

Let's not fool ourselves: you and I both believe in the existence of the world. Each and every one of us demonstrates our belief in the existence of the world several times a day. Not so much when somebody throws a punch and I dodge it, because that person's fist could still exist only in my mind; when it gets too close to the illusion of my body, and causes me pain, that does nothing to disrupt the mental hypothesis. More so, though, when we feel convinced that other people exist, other thinking subjects, and when we are able to empathize with their highs and lows. This is not, of course, proof of the existence of reality, but, rather, proof of how strongly we believe in the existence of reality. And that is even more the case on all the days when we don't commit suicide, when we don't take our own lives just to see if that changes the rules and all of this was merely one of the possible games.

Very well, friendly reader, it is important to note that our modest summary here began with a lie. And that everybody else, from here on out, will therefore be fictional.

We are fictional creatures, metaphorical creatures, and every attempt to know ourselves or to understand the world we have constructed ought to begin with this. Perhaps the only possible thing, consequently, is for us

1 Jorge Luis Borges, 'Olaf Stapledon', *Philosophy and Living* (1940).

to try to impose a little order on the fictions we come up with.

In *The Self and Its Brain* (1977), Karl Popper proposes a tripartite division of the world that might help to provide some organizing principles. Popper broke reality down into: world 1, which corresponds with physical entities, like rocks, trees, gravity and my body; world 2, which includes mental states, such as awareness, individual feelings or the specific effort the mind makes in this moment to interpret these words; and world 3, which takes in the contents of thought, the products of human minds – and among these would be found geology, botany, the law of gravity, the theory of relativity, language, cultural prejudice, macroeconomic crises, unicorns, Cupid, neurology, God, werewolves and Frankenstein's monster. These three worlds interact on a constant basis. On the one hand, my mind connects to things through my sensory experience, which itself supposedly arises in a concrete physical and biological entity that we call the body (world 1 and world 2). On the other, our minds produce ideas that are partially autonomous and may come back around and have far-reaching effects on us. Not only because the things I read and learn transform me every day, but because an economic crisis or a religious dogma can destroy my mental state or even end my life (world 2 and world 3). And, finally, there is also an interaction between ideas and things, because the former either cannot exist without the latter, have an underlying substance or layer in physical objects – think books or computer servers – or because they reside in the networks that are our brains. To varying degrees of complexity, they are in both worlds at the same time: the work of art exists, for example, as a sculpture, but its artistic connotation belongs to the dimension of culture and imagination. Fantastical creatures can even have an impact on the physical world: Frankenstein's monster has given rise not only to works of literature and film, but also to fancy-dress outfits, T-shirts, keyrings, cups and other kinds of merchandise, and to piles of physical books, videotapes and DVDs, as well as festivals and the odd theme park (world 3 and world 1).

The numerical order assigned by Popper is very much intentional. For the Austrian philosopher, the first thing to arise is the physical world, and this in turn gives occasion to the world of the mind, rather than the other way around. Of course, this could very well be so. But to take it as a given and refute the possibility of a causal relationship in the opposite direction is actually groundless, and ultimately comes down to a matter of faith. Despite this – though grudgingly – I will stick to his original denomination in trust that it doesn't become confused in the following exposition.

The first thing to arise is the self and its attendant thought processes.

The first thing is therefore world 2. Not the entire agglomeration of minds we will ultimately include in world 2, though, but, rather, the vanishingly small thing that is my individual self.

The next thing, given that I am possessed of symbolic thought, will be metaphor. The mental image of the world, the awareness of reality, the original lie. From which it follows that world 1 will have taken shape in my mind.

I will assume the exterior existence of my mental images, no more than a hypothesis though this may be, and I will become aware of my own existence as part of this reality. I will include myself in this representation and, what is more, do so in a manner that is very specific and distinctly human, and that allows me to come back finally to a question I raised in the second chapter of this book.

In 'Minus Six', we spoke of the loop, leap or circle entailed by self-referentiality. Our disquisition was then interrupted, but it is now necessary to return to it and establish its limits and boundaries, in order that we can proceed – and particularly to distinguish it from other kinds of awareness. The idea that human beings are the only animals with an awareness of self and of the world is a fallacy. An enormous number of species have recourse to metaphor, and have their own mental image and awareness of reality. Almost all of them, however, remain stuck in the first metaphorical leap – the transformation of the nervous impulse into images – and never make the consequent move into language. But a horse remembers, a cat dreams, and they do so via mental metaphors. And when an iguana is lying in the sun and, spying a predator, suddenly jumps in the water, it is 100 per cent aware that the world around it is more than just itself. By the same token, elephants and chimpanzees recognize themselves in the mirror. Nonetheless, humans are the only creatures – though the notion of intelligence is a question of gradation, and the dividing line between species is not as hard and fast as we like to think – capable of elaborating a metaphor *about* the metaphor. Our propensity for this loop, for talking about what we talk about, our capacity for shifting up to a level above basic language, not only leads us into logical and semantic paradoxes such as the unreliable narrator – this faculty for shifting up into metalanguage also makes it possible for us to be so very self-aware.

Then, after the primary metaphor or after the awareness of the world, we elaborate another meta-metaphor that consists of knowing that we are both part of the world and thinking about the world. Self-referentiality consists of this metaphor for the metaphor. And this – nothing but this – is a purely kind of human awareness.

Of course, we could go on shifting upwards from this level, and think about ourselves in the same way as somebody thinks about creatures who think they are thinking – and many of our rational processes are like this. But this usually gets us lost. And leads us to notice that we lack something as an intelligent species, a qualitative leap that is probably beyond us even to imagine. In the same way, horses, cats and iguanas haven't the first idea what you and I are talking about.

And then, at last, with my own awareness constructed and finalized, I can move on to conceding everybody else's existence. Once I begin projecting world 1 and am furnished with an image of my own mind as part of this exterior world, I can suppose that all those creatures who seem to be the same as me on the outside ought similarly to resemble me in their respective inner worlds. And, on this basis, I make conjectures about their minds, thereby putting the finishing touches to world 2.

This, however, is a new concession. From the point of view of my subjectivity, everyone else's mental states don't belong in world 2 as definitively as Popper seems to believe, but rather belong to all the world 3 effects. This becomes clearer still in the case of all those people of whom I have no empirical impression: somebody living in Ghana, a Chinese person named Yu Martín Xu – these to me are just as fictional as Hitler or Van Gogh, whose rightful place, once they have disappeared from worlds 1 and 2 (along with the now-deceased philosopher Karl Popper), ought to be world 3. And though this might seem like mere metaphysics, in fact it is a cognitive defect very present in our lives and that goes a long way to explaining xenophobia, the immigration policies of certain governments, and even large-scale genocide. It isn't possible for us to empathize with people we perceive merely as concepts. In the same way that for you, reader, I am nothing more than a hazy idea vaguely sketched in your mind.

All that remains, once we have got to this stage in our fictionalizing process, is to go on constructing world 3. Which is exactly the task in which we are all involved.

World 3 is more complex now than ever before in history, due to the fact it encompasses, among other things, almost every other historical period's knowledge. For primitive man, world 3 must have been the smallest by some way, while world 1 – little more than the nearby stretch of sea, the mountains, the sun, the sky, the occasional storm – would have seemed infinite and ungraspable. How insignificant world 3 must have felt, stripped of all its vaporous contraptions. Whereas, in the present day, however much we are told that the universe contains 2 billion galaxies and measures at least 91,000 million light years, these facts still immediately become part of world 3 for us, which grows inexorably larger above our heads all the time. As we have already seen, our immediate environment is so affected by this fictitious world that hyperreality threatens to crush us.

World 3 takes all.

The greatest challenge, caught as we are in this vortex of fictions, may now be to keep our thinking selves in some sort of balance.

The first step may therefore be to recognize that we are by nature fictional creatures.

As a human activity, art is superior to religion, precisely because it recognizes its own fictitiousness. And science would do well to get down from its self-appointed altar and recognize that it works in the realm of the hypothetical – not that certain of its theories are hypothetical, but the entire scientific corpus, because that is as far as human beings are able to go and there is not a single scientist in the world who is able to reach – or even to define – this fiction that we call the truth.

Exactly the same thing happens with certain other manifestations of human grandeur, such as love and altruism. Love is a fiction: sexual and amorous relations are part of the species' plans and bear little resemblance to what we believe we are feeling. Altruism, as suggested by Paul Rée in *Psychological Observations* (1875), is nothing more than a human behaviour that has been reinforced by natural selection over the centuries. Then again, if we believe we are feeling something, doesn't that mean we are really feeling it? In the same way that I may not just be any of my single neurons, but still have a clear and distinct perception of my own thoughts, isn't love a *real* lie for me? Even if it is a deception on the part of biology, aren't the pain and pleasure it produces in my subjectivity genuine?

If we admit their fictitious nature, we will in a Nietzschean sense be transcending these values in order to go one step further. Because when one is conscious of the deception, and still agrees to carry on playing, one is not just a victim. Just as the artist is not only a liar, and the audience member or reader is not only a dupe. It is possible to know the facts, know that our entire chemistry is part of a strategy, that everything I feel actually has another goal, and still to shout: 'Yes, okay everything is a lie! But I love it!' In fiction and in health.

This perspective puts our solipsistic departure point in a considerably different light. Because now, rather than some unsuspecting sap taken in by the great charade, I am an actor who has chosen to act.

> If there even is a natural being – an irreducible self – it is rather small, I think, and may even be the root of all impersonation: the natural being may be the skill itself, the innate capacity to impersonate. I'm talking about recognizing that one is acutely a performer, rather than swallowing whole the guise of naturalness and pretending that it isn't a performance but you.[2]

Everything around us is fake; everything that gives form to our lives and our world is woven from lies. Long before we arrived on the planet, nature was already making use of deceit in its own plans.

Somehow, lies have found a way of slotting into the process of natural selection – of giving an edge. And this has had innumerable repercussions. Us, to begin with: the fictional creatures par excellence, modelled by Darwinian selection to be the epitome of lying. And, going a step further, all human activity as well. If we bear in mind that deception has its origins in the pre-human natural world, perhaps it will be easier for us to comprehend why natural selection has always been the principal organizing agent in all human ambits: something that isn't the case, for example, in the orders of geology or astronomy. Nonetheless, lying and the selective processes of competition, adaptation and survival have always gone hand in hand and are present in every aspect of our society. Not only in human beings' biological patterns, the evolution of the species or our own organism – natural selection, I mean, can also be an organizing criterion in group dynamics; in the formation of societies; in the survival or disappearance of cultures; in the persistence of ethical values; in barter and exchange; in the

---

[2] Philip Roth, *The Counterlife*, London: Vintage, 2005.

microeconomy; in finance, international markets, publicity and marketing; in fashions; in technological progress; and, in general, in all the disciplines and activities that involve the participation of ideas.

As evolutionary epistemology was able to discern, even our own minds have certain innate cognitive mechanisms that are the result of evolution. Certain of our sensory conditions and categories are a priori genetically inherited, quite independent of individual experience, while others are the result of the species's experiences, both positive and negative, over the course of millions of years. This means that our way of thinking and of seeing the world is what it is – and, indeed, could just as easily have been otherwise – due purely to certain random processes in selection. So our inclination for distorting things and for the phantasmagorical is nothing but an accident.

But if we go still further, ideas themselves – and so all the lies – also evolve both separately from our physiology and beyond our control. Even more so since they have been flying around untethered in world 3.

A fiction always needs something to undergird it. This could be a physical object in world 1: a book, a canvas, a blackboard, a warehouse; or indeed a human mind in world 2. In very small communities, before the invention of writing, it must have been very easy for ideas to be snuffed out, and it must have taken a long time for a lie or a legend to be forged that was capable of resisting the vicissitudes of the minds of various groups. Nowadays, however, all the different ways of recording things have combined with the mushrooming global population and the communication networks that connect us to turn the situation on its head. Someone can generate an idea in their mind, and the very next second it can have ceased to belong to them and be out there replicating all across the world. The individual creator of an idea can disappear, and the idea survive for years or centuries. The invention of writing meant increased autonomy for culture, but in our time electronic communication networks – social networks, forums, messaging apps –and all the other communication media have turned our minds into a kind of network between equals (peer-to-peer), that keeps all the ideas and all the lies constantly online.

World 2 has transformed into a network at the disposal of the ideas proper to world 3. Human beings are at the service of ideas, and the individual is starting to become disposable.

We might sometimes be overtaken by the feeling that, somehow, ideas have always been the only thing that matters. Lies were around long before we showed up. And now, all these fictions seem to have evolved and to be following their own path, wherever its destination may be. Independent of us, who have been relegated to mere undergirding.

And this need not necessarily be a bad thing: ideas propagate through us, we fictional beings, as though they were the true living beings.

And perhaps that is true.

Perhaps, once the illusion of identity has been transcended, the only thing that matters will be the ideas we leave behind.

Perhaps the day will come when our species is good for something.

BIBLIOGRAPHY

Arendt, Hannah. *Crises of the Republic: Lying in Politics; Civil Disobedience; On Violence; Thoughts on Politics and Revolution*. Boston: Mariner Books, 1972.

Aristotle. *Poetics*. London: Penguin Classics, 1996.

Augustine, Saint. *The Retractions*. Washington, DC: Catholic University of America Press, 1968 (includes 'On Lying' and 'Against Lying').

Barthes, Roland. *Writing Degree Zero*. London: Vintage, 2010.

Baudrillard, Jean. *Simulacra and Simulation*. Ann Arbor: University of Michigan Press, 1995.

Baudrillard, Jean. *The Perfect Crime*. London: Verso, 2008.

Bentham, Jeremy. *Bentham's Theory of Fictions*. London: Routledge, 2007.

Berger, Peter. *Sacred Canopy: Elements of a Sociological Theory of Religion*. New York: Anchor Books, 1990.

Borges, Jorge Luis. *Collected Fictions*. New York: Penguin Books, 1999.

Borges, Jorge Luis, Bioy Casares, and Silvina Ocampo. *The Book of Fantasy*. London: Viking/Penguin, 1988.

Calderón de la Barca, Pedro. *La vida es sueño / Life is a Dream: A Dual-Language Book*. New York: Dover Publications Inc, 2003.

Calvin, John. *A Treatise on Relics*. Amherst, NY: Prometheus Books, 2009.

Caro Baroja, Julio. *Las falsificaciones de la historia* [The Falsifications of History]. Barcelona: Seix Barral, 1992.

Carroll, Lewis, John Tenniel and Leonard S. Marcus. *The Complete Works of Lewis Carroll*. New York: Barnes & Noble Books, 2005.

Casares, Bioy. *The Invention of Morel*. New York Review of Books, 2003.

Colditz, Jason B., Leila M. Giles, Beth L. Hoffman, et al. 'Association between Social Media Use and Depression', *Depression and Anxiety* 33.4 (2016), pp. 257–64.

Derrida, Jacques. *Writing and Difference*. London: Routledge, 2001.

Descartes, René. *A Discourse on Method*. London: J. M. Dent, 1969.

Dick, Philip K. *Selected Stories of Philip K. Dick*. New York: Houghton Mifflin Harcourt, 2013.

Diogenes, Laertius. *Lives of Eminent Philosophers*. Cambridge University Press, 2017.

Durkheim, Émile. *The Elementary Forms of the Religious Life*. London: Allen & Unwin, 1976.

Eccles, John C., and Karl Popper. *The Self and Its Brain: An Argument for Interactionism*. London: Routledge, 1984.

Eco, Umberto. *The Role of the Reader: Explorations in the Semiotics of Texts*. Bloomington: Indiana University Press, 1984.

Eco, Umberto. *Faith in Fakes*. London: Vintage, 1995.

Eliade, Mircea. *A History of Religious Ideas*. University of Chicago Press, 1988.

Ferré, Juan Francisco. *Providence*. Barcelona: Anagrama, 2009.

Ferré, Juan Francisco. *El rey del juego* [The King of the Game]. Barcelona: Anagrama, 2015.

Feuerbach, Ludwig. *Thoughts on Death and Immortality*. Oakland: University of California Press, 1981.

Feuerbach, Ludwig. *The Essence of Christianity*. New York: Prometheus Books, 1989.

Feyerabend, Paul. *Against Method*. London: Verso, 1988.

Foucault, Michel. *History of Madness*. London: Routledge, 2009.

Foucault, Michel. *The Foucault Reader*. London: Penguin, 2020.

Frankfurt, Harry G. *On Bullshit*. Princeton University Press, 2005.

Freeman, Charles. *A New History of Early Christianity*. New Haven: Yale University Press, 2009.

Freud, Sigmund. *Civilisation and Its Discontents*. London: Hogarth Press and the Institute of Psycho-Analysis, 1975.

Freud, Sigmund. *The Interpretation of Dreams*. Oxford University Press, 2008.

Freud, Sigmund, and Philip Rieff. *General Psychological Theory: Papers on Metapsychology*. New York: Touchstone, 2008.

Gubern, Roman. *Del bisonte a la realidad virtual: la escena y el laberinto* [From the Bison to Virtual Reality: The Scene and the Labyrinth]. Barcelona: Anagrama, 1996.

Hofstadter, Douglas R. *Gödel, Escher, Bach*. London: Penguin, 2000.

Hume, David. *Enquiries Concerning the Human Understanding and Concerning the Principles of Morals*. Westport, CT: Greenwood Press, 1980.

Hume, David. *An Abstract of a Treatise of Human Nature 1740: A Pamphlet Hitherto Unknown*. Bristol: Thoemmes Antiquarian Books, 1990.

Hume, David. *On Suicide*. London: Penguin, 2005.

Hume, David. *Principal Writings on Religion, Including Dialogues Concerning Natural Religion and the Natural History of Religion*. Oxford University Press, 2008.

Jameson, Fredric. *Postmodernism: or, the Cultural Logic of Late Capitalism*. London: Verso Books, 2019.

Kant, Immanuel. *The Critique of Pure Reason; the Critique of Practical Reason: and Other Ethical Treatises; the Critique of Judgement*. Chicago: Encyclopædia Britannica, 2007.

Koyré, Alexandre. *Reflexiones sobre la mentira* [Reflections on Lying]. Buenos Aires: Leviatán, 2004.

Kuhn, Thomas S. *The Structure of Scientific Revolutions*. University of Chicago Press, 1970.

Lem, Stanisław. *Imaginary Magnitude*. London: Mandarin, 1991.

Lem, Stanisław. *A Perfect Vacuum*. Evanston, IL: Northwestern University Press, 1999.

Lem, Stanisław. *Stanislaw Lem: Biography, Letters, Provocation*. Liverpool University Press, 2014.

Lem, Stanisław. *Summa technologiae*. Minneapolis: University of Minnesota Press, 2014.

Lévi-Strauss, Claude. *The Savage Mind*. University of Chicago Press, 1969.

Lévi-Strauss, Claude. *Structural Anthropology*. London: Penguin Books, 1994.

Lévy, Pierre. *Cyberculture*. Minneapolis: University of Minnesota Press, 2001.

Loiperdinger, Martín. 'Lumiere's Arrival of the Train: Cinema's Founding Myth', *Moving Image* 4.1 (2004).

Lynch, Enrique. *Filosofía y/o literatura. Identidad y/o diferencia* [Philosophy and/or Literature: Identity and/or Difference]. Buenos Aires: Fondo de Cultura Económica, 2007.

Machiavelli, Niccolò. *The Prince*. Oxford University Press, 2008.

Maillard, Chantal. *La creación por la metáfora: introducción a la razón-poética* [Creation by Metaphor: Introduction to Poetic-Reason]. Barcelona: Anthropos, 1992.

Marx, Karl. *Das Kapital*. London: Penguin Classics, 1992.

Marx, Karl, Friedrich Engels and Roy Pascal. *The German Ideology*. Mansfield, CT: Martino Publishing, 2011.

Molina Mejía, Andrés. *El pensamiento moderno: Descartes* [Modern Thought: Descartes]. Malaga: Ágora, 1993.

Muñoz Rengel, Juan Jacinto. 'De la crítica estructuralista a la disolución de la estética, el lenguaje y la realidad' [On the Structuralist Critique of the Dissolution of Aesthetics, Language and Reality], *Anthropos* 186 (1998), pp. 103–7.

Muñoz Rengel, Juan Jacinto. '¿En qué creía Borges?' [What Did Borges Believe In?], *Iberomania* (University of Tübingen, Germany) 51 (1999), pp. 91–104.

Muñoz Rengel, Juan Jacinto. 'Los apriorismos kantianos' [Kantian Apriorisms], *Revista de Filosofía* (Complutense University of Madrid) 9.21 (1999), pp. 143–68.

Muñoz Rengel, Juan Jacinto. *El sueño del otro* [The Dream of the Other]. Barcelona: Plaza & Janés, 2013.

Muñoz Rengel, Juan Jacinto. 'Tres siglos de mentiras políticas' [Three Centuries of Political Lies], *El País*, 28 May 2013, p. 31.

Muñoz Rengel, Juan Jacinto. 'Lo fantástico como indagación. La ficción como herramienta del conocimiento' [The Fantastical as Inquiry: Fiction as a Tool for Knowledge], in N. Alvarez Mendez and A. Abello Verano, eds., *Espejismos de la realidad* [Mirages of Reality]. University of Leon Press, 2015.

Nietzsche, Friedrich. *Thus Spake Zarathustra*. London: Penguin Classics, 1974.

Nietzsche, Friedrich. *Beyond Good and Evil*. London: Penguin Classics, 2003.

Nietzsche, Friedrich. *On Truth and Lies in a Nonmoral Sense*. London: Harper Perennial Modern Classics, 2010.

Nietzsche, Friedrich. *On Truth and Untruth: Selected Writings*. London: Harper Perennial Modern Classics, 2010.

Nietzsche, Friedrich. *The Joyous Science*. London: Penguin Classics, 2018.

Penrose, Roger. *Shadows of the Mind: A Search for the Missing Science of Consciousness*. Oxford University Press, 1994.

Penrose, Roger. *The Emperor's New Mind: Concerning Computers, Minds, and the Laws of Physics*. Oxford University Press, 2016.

Plutarch. *Greek Lives*. Oxford University Press, 2008.

Popper, Karl. *The Logic of Scientific Discovery*. London: Routledge Classics, 2002.

Ricœur, Paul. *Freud and Philosophy: An Essay on Interpretation*. New Haven: Yale University Press, 1971.

Russell, Bertrand. *The Analysis of Mind*. London: George Allen & Unwin, 1921.

Russell, Bertrand. *An Outline of Philosophy*. London: Routledge, 2009.

Russell, Bertrand. *Why I Am Not a Christian*. London: Routledge, 2017.

Saussure, F. *Course in General Linguistics*. London: Duckworth, 1993.

Schmitt, Jean-Claude. *Historia de la superstición* [History of Superstition]. Barcelona: Crítica, 1992.

Schopenhauer, Arthur. *The World as Will and Idea*. London: Phoenix, 1995.

Scudéry, Madeleine. *Choix de conversations de Mlle de Scudéry*. Ravenna: Longo, 2002.

Simmel, Georg. *The Sociology of Sociability*. Indianapolis: Bobbs-Merrill, College Division, 1960.

Sun Tzu. *The Art of War*. San Diego: Canterbury Classics, 2014.

Swift, Jonathan. *A Modest Proposal and Other Writings*. London: Alma Classics, 2019.

Tinasky, Guillermo. *La ofensa* [The Offence]. Barcelona: Malpaso, 2017.

Vaihinger, Hans. *The Philosophy of 'As If'*. Abingdon, Oxon.: Routledge, Taylor & Francis Group, 2021.

Weber, Max. *Science as a Vocation*. Indianapolis: Bobbs-Merrill, College Division, 1960.

Wilde, Oscar. *The Decay of Lying*. London: Penguin Books, 2020.

Wittgenstein, Ludwig. *Philosophical Investigations*. Oxford: Blackwell, 1992.

Wittgenstein, Ludwig. *Tractatus Logico-Philosophicus: Centenary Edition*. London: Anthem Press, 2021.

Žižek, Slavoj. *The Plague of Fantasies*. London: Verso, 2009.